College Roommate Essentials on How To Talk To Anyone

The Ultimate Survival Guide to
How to Have Roommates
That Don't Suck!

Faith Fuson

Copyright © 2023 by Faith Fuson

All rights reserved.

The content contained within this book may not be reproduced, duplicated, or transmitted without direct written permission from the author or publisher. Under no circumstances will any blame or legal responsibility be held against the publisher, or author, for any damages, reparation, or monetary loss due to the information contained within this book, either directly or indirectly.

Legal Notice: This book is copyright protected. It is only for personal use. You cannot amend, distribute, sell, use, quote or paraphrase any part, or the content within this book, without the consent of the author or publisher.

Disclaimer Notice: Please note the information contained within this document is for educational and entertainment purposes only. All effort has been executed to present accurate, up-to-date, reliable, and complete information. No warranties of any kind are declared or implied. Readers acknowledge that the author is not engaged in the rendering of legal, financial, medical, or professional advice. The content within this book has been derived from various sources. Please consult a licensed professional before attempting any techniques or contract outlined in this book. By reading this document, the reader agrees that under no circumstances is the author responsible for any losses, direct or indirect, that are incurred as a result of the use of the information contained within this document, including, but not limited to, errors, omissions, or inaccuracies.

Transparent Moment: Some, not all, of the links you click on in this book are affiliate links. Why? Well, let's be real - I'm shamelessly using them to help pay for my daughter's college education and those pesky student loans. So, while you're getting awesome content, you're also secretly becoming my accomplice in sending my kid to college. It's a win-win, right? Thanks for being a part of this exciting, college-financing adventure!

Dedication

To my incredible daughter and her amazing roommates, who have unknowingly become the muses behind this book. You four have inspired me with your unique blend of chaos, laughter, and questionable food choices. May the tales of your college adventures serve as a guide to set you up for success in the wild realm of roommating.

Here's to late-night cram sessions, random dance parties, and the unforgettable memories we're about to make.

Cheers, my fearless scholars!

Contents

Introduction 1

First, Know Thyself 11

Getting Started and
Moving In 23

Establishing Mutual
Expectations for Shared Living 33

Establishing Healthy
Patterns of Communication 55

About Personality Types 61

The Myers-Briggs Personality Types
as Roommates 71

And What About Me? How Can I Be the Best
Roommate Given My Personality Type? 109

Communication Styles and Skills 139

How To Address Tensions and Resolve Conflicts 163

Final Words 183

Bonus Content 185

Faith Fuson

Introduction

Why live together?

IN LATE 2022, The Wall Street Journal reported that skyrocketing rental prices in America had risen 25% in the prior two years. Along with inflation in the prices of food and household goods, as well as other costs of living, expenses today exceed what many renters living alone can afford. As a result, many renters of all ages are choosing to share housing with roommates rather than live alone. It has become much too difficult to take on these rising costs alone.

A recent article in Forbes noted a significant spike in the demand for home-sharing situations, citing a Harvard study that showed an 88% rise in adult cohabitating between 2006-2016. This is a phenomenon that continues to rise, especially following the sense of social isolation that characterized the COVID pandemic years.

Urban planning scholar Sophia Maalsen at The University of Sydney in Australia studies the way housing trends are being reconfigured, dubbing the current generation as "Generation Share." As home ownership declines and renting increases, the phenomenon of shared housing is becoming a norm. She argues that people are sharing housing for longer periods—no longer just as transitional places to live between leaving the family home and buying a home of their own.

Maalsen notes a widening age demographic among those sharing homes, since many people choose to share a home not only for economic but also for emotional and physical safety reasons as they seek mutual support and companionship.

Clearly, a roommate guide like this one isn't just relevant to college students anymore. In this new era of collaborate living, everyone from college freshmen to silver-haired seniors are sharing homes.

In this book, I introduce the concept of a roommate or housemate as a distinct kind of relationship: not exactly family, not necessarily good friends, but not a typical business relationship, either. Sharing your living space with another person incurs a degree of intimacy, because you're exposing the more private side of yourself to another person.

However, the relationship of house-sharers is also based on a reciprocal respect for maintaining mutually agreed-upon boundaries and considering each other's needs and desires. Far from effortless, it requires ongoing attention and the building of new types of relational skills.

Never assume that you already know how to be a great roommate—becoming an optimal roomie to each person you live with is an ongoing learning process that you'll need to adapt to in each new living situation.

Throughout this book, I assume a primary dyadic (two-person) living situation. This can include living with a college roommate, whether chosen or assigned, or sharing an apartment or house with either a stranger or a casual friend.

If you live with more than one other person, you'll not only have a dyadic relationship with each of them, but also the added complexity of group dynamics. While I allude to multiple housemates here and there throughout the book, I do not address the issues of group dynamics here.

The Significance of College Roommates

Much research in the social sciences focuses on the importance of roommates, with a frequent focus on the freshman college experience and the primary role it can play in shaping a student's post-secondary school reality. Below, a few reasons why roommate relationships can be so influential:

When you live with someone, you spend a lot of time together and share a living space. This can create a close bond, but it can also lead to conflicts and tension.

Roommates can provide social support during the often-stressful first-year college experience. They can offer emotional support, a listening ear, or the role of a study partner.

Living with a roommate can be a learning experience in itself as you learn about different lifestyles, cultures, and perspectives. This can broaden your horizons and help you become more open-minded.

Your roommate may be the person who shares many of your college experiences with you, such as attending events or parties, studying for exams, or exploring the campus.

Essentially, college roommate relationships can shape your collegiate experiences either positively or negatively, depending upon how well you learn to cope with living with someone outside your own family.

Whether you're an 18-year-old college freshman (our archetypal roommate situation), a professional in your 20s or 30s who's sharing a flat or apartment with another person, or a widowed retiree who's decided to move in with a friend to avoid living alone and to save money in your golden years, this book will provide you with valuable insights.

Emotional Intelligence and Interpersonal Communication Skills

Throughout these chapters, I address a range of interpersonal communication skills that you can develop to help your roommate relationship thrive, as well as to learn to resolve budding conflicts before they become emotionally painful.

You'll find that my approach stems from an emphasis on developing emotional intelligence and interpersonal communication skills as the foundation for developing and maintaining healthy, happy, and mutually satisfying roommate relationships. I emphasize the role of self-awareness and managing your own emotions as you learn to recognize and respect your roommate's emotions. Ultimately, it comes down to honing your skills in balancing emotional and logical thinking in your decision making.

Emotional intelligence (EI, sometimes called EQ to compare it to IQ) is the ability to understand and manage your own emotions and to recognize and respond to the emotions of other people. It plays a crucial role in our interpersonal relationships, as it helps us to communicate effectively, empathize with others, and navigate social situations with greater ease.

Some aspects of emotional intelligence that will be of great use in a house-sharing situation include:

Developing your emotional intelligence will help you to understand your own emotions, strengths, weaknesses, and biases. In doing so, you'll build self-awareness and cultivate self-improvement, which are crucial for healthy and fulfilling relationships.

Emotional intelligence enables you to communicate effectively with others by recognizing and responding appropriately to the emotions being expressed. This can help you build trust, rapport, and mutual understanding in your relationships.

EI also enables you to put yourself in someone else's shoes and understand their emotions, thoughts, and experiences. Doing so builds empathy and compassion, which are essential for fostering strong and meaningful relationships.

Your emotional intelligence will also help you manage conflicts in a constructive and positive manner. It enables you to stay calm, listen to others' perspectives, and find mutually beneficial solutions to the problem at hand.

In short, making an effort to further develop your emotional intelligence will be critical as you build and maintain strong interpersonal relationships, whether in personal or professional settings.

Bad Roommates—or Poor Communication?

If you read memes, online listicles, or magazine articles about "roommates gone wild," you may come away with the impression that getting a good roommate or a bad roommate is just the luck of the draw. According to popular culture, bad roommates are like rotten apples that you need to toss out and replace with shiny, fresh ones.

Below, some common examples of stories frequently found online about stereotypical bad roommates:

The messy roommate: This is perhaps the most common type of bad roommate. They leave dirty dishes in the sink, leave clothes and belongings scattered everywhere, and rarely clean up after themselves. This can, understandably, lead to an unpleasant and unsanitary living environment.

The noisy roommate: Whether it's playing loud music, having guests over late at night, or talking on the phone loudly, a noisy roommate can make it difficult to sleep, study, or relax at home.

The moocher roommate: This roommate never contributes their fair share to household expenses, such as rent, utilities, or groceries. They may also borrow your things without asking or never offer to help with chores.

The passive-aggressive roommate: This type avoids confrontation, and instead communicates their frustrations through notes, text messages, or other indirect means. They may also leave flippant messages about chores or make snide remarks about your behavior.

The inconsiderate roommate: This type of roommate doesn't take into account how their actions affect others in the household. They may take long showers, use up all the hot water, or monopolize the living room TV without considering the needs or desires of others.

These are just a few examples of the types of unsavory roommates that you may encounter. But my approach to these problems is not to write any of these stereotypical roommates off as terrible people you should never live with. Each of these roommate types is not necessarily "bad"; they're likely just living according to their personality type and their preferences.

Until they become aware of how their preferred behavior affects you, and until you come up with mutually agreed-upon guidelines and expectations for how you can live together, they may seem like undesirable roommates, but that doesn't mean that you two are necessarily incompatible.

In chapters 5 to 7, I explain a system for determining your personality type (and your roommate's, if you can persuade them to take the test). Some of these stereotypes may not even sound that bad to you, depending upon your own personality type.

However frustrating and stressful dealing with a so-called "bad roommate" can be, you're likely to improve the living situation with another person by setting clear boundaries, communicating effectively, and seeking outside help (if necessary). Don't expect any roommate to be a perfect fit from the first day you move in together. As I explain throughout the book, developing a strong roommate relationship takes effort—but it will turn out to be well worth it!

Improved communication has a significant positive impact on roommate relationships. It can:

- help build trust between you and your roommate. When you communicate clearly and openly, you're more likely to be seen as reliable and trustworthy.
- help you address problems or conflicts that arise between you and your roommate. When you feel comfortable expressing your concerns, you can work together to find solutions that work for both of you.
- enhance empathy, which is the ability to understand and share the feelings of others. When you communicate well with your roommate, you're more likely to understand their perspective and be able to empathize with them.
- help ensure that the living conditions are comfortable and accommodating for both of you. You can discuss your preferences for cleanliness, noise levels, and other factors that affect your living environment.
- play a role in building a stronger, more positive relationship based on mutual respect and

understanding. This can lead to a happier, more peaceful living situation.

While stereotypes of "the housemate from hell" ring true in many cases—as well as provide a lot of humor, this guide seeks to help you move beyond the stereotyping to try to understand the personality issues involved on both parts when it comes to developing a compatible roommate relationship.

How This Book Can Help You

As you read through the book, you can either approach it by reading from cover to cover or you can skim through it, picking and choosing whichever chapters call out to you. Different readers take different approaches. Below, a brief breakdown of what will be covered:

Chapter 1 is about developing self-awareness as you reflect upon your own values, expectations, style, and needs as a roommate, and considering what kind of a person you might be looking for in a roommate.

Chapter 2 delves into interviewing and finding a compatible roommate. You'll create a Roommate Agreement as your first exercise in learning to communicate well and getting to know each other.

Chapter 3 focuses on establishing mutual expectations for shared living, a continuation of the process you began with the Roommate Agreement.

Chapter 4 continues this process and explores ways to establish healthy patterns of ongoing communication and to create a comfortable practice of having house meetings.

Chapters 5, 6, and 7 form a mini-handbook on how the Myers-Briggs Type Indicator, a personality type assessment, can be extremely useful when you apply it to shared housing relationships. Chapter 5 explains the background of personality typing, and how understanding these types may be useful to you. Chapter 6 looks at different personality types and their possible behaviors as roommates, while Chapter 7 does the same but also looks at your own personality type and what you can bring into a roommate relationship.

Chapter 8 centers on communication styles and skills, and it's a primer on social norms and expectations for civil relationships, some important foundations for developing communicative competence and emotional intelligence, and how to handle some communication problems with a roommate.

Finally, Chapter 9 focuses on how to address and resolve conflicts that will invariably arise between people living together. It provides some steps and processes to help you develop a proactive way to speak with your roommate about problems while they're still small to avoid having them blow up and destroy your relationship.

Faith Fuson

First, Know Thyself

YOU MIGHT BE reading this book because you're just starting the process of trying to find someone to live with. Alternatively, it might be because you're already in a living situation with one or more roommates or housemates—and maybe you need some help learning to live with and get along with them better.

No matter what brought you here, I'm going to provide some tools and insights to help you develop the best relationship possible with the person or persons you live with!

The most common roommate problems, from my experience, arise when one or both roommates thinks that good roommates are born that way and need to automatically "fit together perfectly" without any effort on their part. Without putting in an effort to respect, understand, communicate with—and adapt to—a living partner's needs and style of living, your project is doomed from the get-go! Read on as I explain how you can avoid those pitfalls.

Any kind of relationship building is built on the interactions between two people—and that includes you. The first lesson I want you to take away from this book is this: you contribute 50% to having a successful co-living situation. It's your responsibility just as well as that other person's to find a common ground and create the blueprint for how to live together happily.

It's far too easy to blame the other person when things aren't going perfectly. Stories about your crazy or messy or lazy or peculiar roommate can evoke lots of sympathy from your family and friends, I know. I hear them all the time!

But when someone comes to me complaining about problems they're having with a roommate, the first approach I take is to help them understand the dynamics of how each of them interacts with the other. When I get into relationship counseling mode, my role isn't just to listen and sympathize about what a bad roommate someone feels they have or how they just drew the wrong name in the lottery.

Instead, my approach (and this book) is based on the premise that nearly any two people can learn to develop a fruitful working relationship with each other when they are sharing a living space. Read that again! Finding a good roommate isn't like trying on clothes to see which ones fit or look best on you. You don't need to keep trying out and rejecting housemates until you find someone who feels like your best friend.

Instead, whether you have a roommate assigned to you (as many college and university students do), you move in with a friend of a friend, or you find a housemate through a classified ad on a roommate site or Craigslist, the key to living together successfully is in learning to be a considerate and thoughtful co-habitator who:

- uses excellent communication skills
- realizes that each person (yes, that includes you!) needs to always be willing to give and take
- most importantly, understands that being roommates doesn't necessarily mean being close friends

The Roommate Relationship

Being a roommate or housemate might be a new kind of relationship you've never been in before. It's like a business relationship (think about how you interact with coworkers, classmates, or hobby groups), but it's different because it involves a lot more personal exposure and intimacy—which means learning to be your best self even when you're at home chilling and aren't wearing any of the masks we wear "out in the world" at our jobs or as students.

My opening proposition to you then is to *adjust your expectations of what your relationship with a roommate or housemate needs to be.* You don't need to be soulmates. You don't need to like the same kinds of music or eat the same types of food. You may come from completely different family or cultural backgrounds.

But *your mission is to get along well enough to respectfully share the same living space*—whether it's a dorm room, an apartment, or an entire house. You need to be kind and respectful to each other. You need to tolerate each other's eccentricities without getting too annoyed. You need to respect each other's privacy. You both need to be willing to communicate with each other about your expectations and come to agreements about mutual expectations, which will likely require some give-and-take negotiations. Most of all, you need to be willing to put in the work to understand each other's personality types so that you can learn to live together conflict-free.

This may sound like a lot of work, but no relationships come pre-made. If you can master the relationship-building skills to become a great roommate, then you'll have some pretty important life skills that will help you out in lots of other situations in life, too.

What Kind of Roommate Are You? Your Habits and Customs

What kind of a roommate or housemate are you or will you be? The most fundamental part of becoming a great roommate is to know yourself. It's surprising how many of us think, *"Of course I know who I am!"* But it's not at all surprising that many young people—and this book will probably be most relevant to those from 18 who are just leaving their family home up through those in their 30s who are sharing homes with others—don't self-reflect about what they bring into a co-housing relationship.

To start with, many of us bring with us the living habits that we've learned in our families growing up. This is especially true for college students. Most of us don't ever examine our own culture until we become immersed in a cultural environment that's different from the one we've been accustomed to. At home, everybody always did things the same way, and that was the way it was.

You may have thought that was just "normal"—which it may have been, for your family. But as you leave home and become exposed to the ways other families from different communities, ethnic groups, states, regions, or nationalities do things, your world grows! And with it grows your expanding awareness of how varied and diverse the people around you truly are.

These "ways of doing things" can range from everyday customs like how you make up your bed, to how and when you eat meals (and what those meals consist of), and to what you think is appropriate personal distance between people. All these customs vary widely, certainly within the United States but especially globally.

For example, growing up a middle class, white American household as I did, each of our raised beds had a soft mattress covered by a fitted sheet, on top of which we laid a flat sheet and perhaps a blanket in colder weather and topped with a bedspread. We had pillows with pillowcases. We slept one person to a single bed, one or two people to a double or queen bed, and each of us children had a desire for our own room if our house was big enough to allow for it. If not, sisters and brothers shared a room.

We had an *ethic of individualism*, so we each had "our" possessions: toys, clothes, books, and so on.

We occasionally shared things, of course, but from an early age we were possessive of what was "mine" and even territorial, maybe telling siblings to "Stay out of my room" or "Don't touch my stuff."

Many families in America (and elsewhere) do not share the norms I just described. Many family cultures are more *collectivist*, which means that they emphasize sharing rather than individual ownership of things. Larger families might fit more children into a bed, so each person's sense of the space they're entitled to is much smaller. If you spend time in parts of Europe, you'll find beds with only a bottom sheet and a comforter (often called a duvet), with no top sheet. In some other parts of the world, people sleep on floor mats or on hard platforms.

Other cultural differences revolve around food, cooking, and eating. You may be accustomed to a large, hot, hearty breakfast with eggs, bacon, sausage, potatoes, toast, and more, while your housemate might be satisfied with a piece of fruit and a cup of yogurt. Your housemate may cook a very different cuisine from the one you grew up with, using different flavors and spices and creating totally new smells and tastes for you. If you experience this, consider how lucky you are to gain exposure to some of the wondrous and diverse cuisines of the world!

While mainstream Americans sit at tables with chairs and eat off of individual plates, in many other cultures families sit on pillows or mats on the floor, with a low table. While we may eat with forks, spoons, and knives, people in other cultures eat with chopsticks, as in Asia, or with their hands, as in Ethiopia, where food is placed on a large table-sized piece of spongy bread called injera, which the diners tear off and use to pick up their other food.

The mindset that will make you the very best roommate or housemate is to enter a new living situation with the anticipation of experiencing and being exposed to new ways of living that will open your mind and habits. Instead of being judgmental or critical about a housemate's ways of doing things (customs and traditions) that aren't like your own, try to approach the new habits with curiosity and an open mind.

If you're a first-time roommate coming directly from living with your family to living with another person, be aware that you're shifting from the roles and expectations you grew up with into a new kind of adult relationship that will expose you to fresh ideas and approaches to life.

Values

In addition to customs, you'll also inevitably encounter people whose values differ from yours. These can be religious or spiritual values, as well as those about what things are more important to prioritize or that you consider to be tied to your sense of morality. Sometimes, we can be exposed to values that make us feel uncomfortable because they're outside our comfort zone. Remember that you can absolutely learn to accept and tolerate your roommate's values without losing your own.

I'm not advocating that you live just as your roommate does. But what's important is to respect a roommate's or housemate's values—even if you don't share them—as long as they're not harming you or doing something illegal. It's all too common for each of us to judge and look down upon those who aren't like ourselves, but your goal should be acceptance and respect of the other person (and the hope that, in turn, they will accept and respect you). This approach will go a long way toward helping you to develop a positive and fulfilling roommate relationship.

When Roommates Have Differences

Below are some examples of situations that illustrate the principles described above.

Brittany, a white college freshman who has grown up in a Southern Baptist (Christian) tradition, moves into a room with A'ishah, a young African American woman who grew up in the Islamic faith. The two roommates will need to learn about each other's cultural and religious practices and respect the differences in how they pray, eat, and live their lives according to the teachings of each of their faiths and backgrounds. Rather than thinking the other is weird, off-base, or some other stereotype, each roommate has the potential to learn a lot about life and the wider world from each other.

Derek, who identifies as part of the LGBTQ community, welcomes Ben, a heterosexual, to share an apartment with him. Initially, Ben feels quite uncomfortable because he's never had a gay friend and doesn't know anything about the queer lifestyle. Ben feels especially fearful that people will think he's gay too, and he's very protective of his masculinity. But as the two get to know each other and realize that even though they're attracted to different genders, they still have a lot of things in common. They begin to understand and become able to respect each other's lifestyles.

Lawrence is a conservative young man living in a house with two housemates. He's always believed in waiting until marriage to have sex, and he takes this very seriously. One of his housemates is a woman, Maggie, who brings boyfriends home to sleep over with her several nights a week. The other housemate doesn't seem to mind, but Lawrence feels that Maggie's hookup culture is disgusting and he has no respect for her, although she's otherwise a very nice person to him. While Lawrence shouldn't be disrespectful of Maggie's sexual decisions, which are her own private concern, the three roommates would benefit from a house meeting to come to an agreement about bringing overnight guests into the house and to discuss safety issues, as well as how having strangers in the house affects the other roommates.

Brita comes from a very warm, talkative, and affectionate large family in which no one has many personal boundaries. She's now living in an apartment with Lillie, an only child who's very introverted and accustomed to having her own space and privacy. Lillie gets really upset when Brita just walks into her room without knocking and starts talking, not taking the hints that Lillie doesn't want to talk right then and there. What's more, Brita is always hugging Lillie and making her cringe—her family members are definitely not huggers. Lillie doesn't like confrontation and doesn't know how to establish her personal boundaries with Brita without upsetting her. Some clear communication is needed.

Even though each of these scenarios presents some discomforting situations between roommates, none of them are situations so severe that they cannot be overcome with self-awareness, a better understanding of the other person, and the development of improved communication. In the following chapters, I'll help you build some skills to help you take leadership in developing a productive relationship with your housemates or roommates.

Let's Get Started

What I recommend you do is get out a notebook, do some self-examination and soul-searching, and make some notes to yourself about your own expectations for your own ability to live with people who are different from you.

What are your biggest worries and fears? What would be the worst-case scenario for you with a roommate? Let's start with this gut feeling. You may come back and make some changes later on, but try to dig down and consider what kinds of differences you think you could tolerate—or even appreciate—as opposed to those that would be absolute no-go situations.

Once you've written some notes on that, let's develop a self-awareness profile. Answer the following questions:

- What's your personality and style?

- What's your cultural and family background?
- Do you embrace that background?
- Are you open to broadening your perspective to other backgrounds?
- What do you anticipate will be your preferred lifestyle and values when you're living with a roommate?
- How open are you to a diversity of lifestyles, cultures, and values?
- What are your eating and food expectations?
- How do you feel about pets?
- How would habits regarding smoking, overnight guests, or a radically different sleeping schedule affect you?
- What are your media habits (including gaming)?
- Are you on the autism spectrum? Do you have ADHD? Any other emotional or physical conditions? Do you take any medications regularly?
- What's your MBTI Personality Type? If you aren't sure, read Chapters 5 to 7 of this book, and arrange to take the Myers-Briggs personality type assessment. This will go a long way toward helping you to understand your own preferences and to better understand your roommate, too.

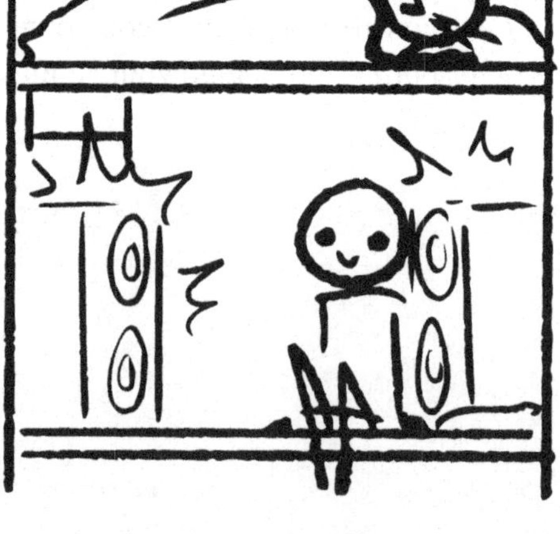

Faith Fuson

Getting Started and Moving In

Finding a Compatible Roommate

In the first chapter, I made the statement that nearly any two people can learn to develop a fruitful working relationship with each other when sharing a living space. That is true, and you may find yourself co-habitating with someone else on a few occasions in your life when you'll need to "love the one you're with," as sung by the 1970s folk rock group Crosby, Stills, Nash, and Young.

You won't always have the opportunity to choose a housemate who's perfect for you; many times, you may either get assigned a roommate or not have the luxury of winnowing down a big list until you find the ideal housing match. In those cases, another way of paraphrasing the lyrics mentioned above would be to "make the best of what you've got." Very few potential roommates are worth discarding altogether. In most cases, unless you just rub each other the wrong way from the moment you meet or you seriously feel afraid of the person when you interview them, you can create a workable relationship.

Of course, creating a workable relationship and finding someone you really feel connected to are two different things, but be sure to keep in mind what I emphasized in Chapter 1: when looking for a roommate, you aren't necessarily looking for a best friend. In fact, living with your best friend isn't always the best idea, as many friendships have ended because of disagreements arising from living together. Just as falling in love with a best friend has the potential to seriously destabilize the good thing you had going, so does living with a best friend. If you can keep your roommate relationship friendly in tone but still remember that it's a working relationship (especially if finances are involved), you may be better off. It really depends upon the personalities involved and how well you can separate the two roles.

If you work through the chapters in this book and take the Myers-Briggs personality type assessment, then study Chapters 5 to 7 of this book to learn more about your own personality type and that of some potential housemates, you should have a profile in mind of the types of roommates who would be most compatible with your personality and lifestyle. With those qualities in mind, you can set out and look for someone to live with.

If you're interviewing strangers, be sure to learn more about them as best you can. Chatting by phone or email is fine to start with, but you need to also meet them face to face. Below, I'll give you a list of questions you might ask. You can also request references, and some people even run background checks, especially in urban areas. Be sure to meet in safe, public places with other people around, or bring a friend if you're visiting a house where someone's advertising for a housemate. We live in an age of online dating and

Craigslist buying and selling, but remember that lots of scammers are out there, so take due diligence.

Finding a Roommate or Housemate

So then, how do you go about finding candidates to live with? You may already have a living space but need a person to move in and share it with you. On the other hand, you may be in a new area, hoping to find a place to live as well as someone to live there with you. Although finding a roommate can be a challenging task, there are several ways to go about it:

1. Word of mouth: Tell your friends, family, and colleagues that you're looking for a roommate. They may know someone who is looking for a place to live.
2. Social media: Post on social media platforms like Facebook, Twitter, and Instagram to let people know that you're looking for a roommate. Be specific about the location, rental budget, and any other requirements.
3. Online roommate matching services: You'll find lots of online services like Roomster, Roomi, and RoomZoom that help match people looking for a roommate.
4. University housing office: If you're a student looking for someone to share an apartment with, your university housing office may be able to help you.
5. Alumni networks: As a graduate of a particular college or university, you may find luck by pursuing local alumni networks. Many of them have city-specific Facebook pages.

6. Classified ads: You can also place an ad in the classified section of your local newspaper (online or in print) or other local publication, as well as on websites like Craigslist.

Interviewing Potential Roommates

When looking for a roommate, it's important to ask them the right questions to ensure that you'll be compatible living together. Some questions to consider asking a potential roommate:

- Tell me about yourself. What are your main interests?
- What are you looking for in a roommate or housemate?
- How long do you plan to stay?
- What is your daily routine like?
- What is your occupation and work schedule?
- What kind of work do you do? Does it provide a reliable income?
- How do you typically spend your free time?
- Do you like to cook? How often do you cook, and what types of foods?
- Are you comfortable with sharing common spaces like the kitchen, living room, and bathroom?
- How do you prefer to handle cleaning and chores?
- Do you have any pets?
- Do you have any allergies?
- Do you smoke cigarettes?
- How much do you drink?
- Do you use cannabis products?
- What are your expectations for guests and visitors? What is your opinion on overnight guests?

- Are you in a romantic relationship?
- What are your sleep habits and preferences?
- How do you typically handle conflicts or disagreements?
- What are challenges you've faced in past living situations?
- Have you ever been arrested or in trouble with the law?
- Anything else I should know?

Ask for phone numbers and email addresses of references. Also, if you are the one looking for someone to live in your apartment or house, ask for proof of income.

It's crucial to develop rapport and establish an open, honest communication with a potential roommate. Don't be afraid to ask additional questions or share your own expectations and preferences for living together.

Red Flags

When interviewing potential roommates, watch out for certain red flags that may indicate they might not be a good fit for you. Below are some common red flags to be aware of, and this is why checking references is so crucial: some of this information you might pick up in an interview, but other issues require a bit of background checking to find out.

- They're unwilling to discuss their daily routine or lifestyle habits.
- They're unwilling to discuss or compromise on sharing common spaces or chores.

- They're unable to provide references or proof of income.
- They seem to be unreliable or have a lack of stability in their life.
- They have a history of not paying rent or bills on time.
- They have a history of substance abuse or addiction.
- They have a criminal history or a history of violence.
- They have a large number of guests or visitors who may disturb your privacy.
- They do not respect your personal boundaries or belongings.
- They have a history of conflict or problematic relationships with previous roommates.

Trust your instincts when meeting potential roommates and pay attention to any red flags that may make you feel uncomfortable or uneasy. Remember, you'll be living with this person, so it's important to choose someone with whom you feel comfortable and who has a compatible lifestyle with you.

Creating a Roommate Agreement

While you'll need a legal document like a lease to cover the issues of financial responsibility in relation to the property and the landlord (and I recommend that each of you have your name on the lease), let's explore the idea of creating a Roommate Agreement that governs the expectations, rights, and obligations that you and your new roommate agree to. This should include house rules, housekeeping and maintenance duties, acceptable and restricted behaviors, and more. It should be a written agreement signed by each person living in the household.

This Roommate Agreement applies to roommates sharing a college dorm room as well as housemates sharing a house or apartment. The roommates should draw it up together and discuss the importance of each item included. I provide a guideline and template here, but your Roommate Agreement can be customized to your particular relationship. By creating and writing out clear expectations that you mutually agree upon, you reduce the risk of having disagreements, which will in turn enhance your relationship so that you can live harmoniously. Even though you'll have a legal contract (a lease) with the landlord, it's important to include the following information in this Roommate Agreement:

1. Your full names
2. The rental property address
3. The date you entered into the agreement
4. An end date for the agreement
5. The total amount of the rent, as well as when and how often it gets paid, and to whom
6. The total amount of the security deposit paid, who paid it (if equally split, say so), and how/when it will be returned
7. The agreed-upon amount of rent each roommate (by name) will pay, by what method, and by what date
8. Specify who will pay what share of household costs and utilities, which may include:

a. gas
b. water
c. Wi-Fi
d. electricity
e. telephone
f. trash removal
g. television service
h. yard maintenance

Rules and conditions for terminating the tenancy:

1. How much notice is needed before one roommate chooses to move out?
2. Under what conditions can one roommate require another roommate to move out?
3. If one roommate moves out or fails to pay their share of rent or bills, how long before the other roommate can find a replacement roommate? What will the remaining roommate do with the departed roommate's abandoned property?
4. Can the remaining roommate ask their landlord for consent to sublease to a new roommate or to amend the lease to include a new tenant?
5. House rules regarding any of the following subjects:

    a. Cleaning and chores (be sure to specify who, what, how often)
    b. How to pay for communal items (shared food, household goods and supplies, utilities)
    c. Pet policy and responsibilities
    d. Firearms
    e. Smoking cigarettes, alcohol, cannabis, other recreational drugs
    f. Quiet hours

g. Guests, or having friends over to hang out
h. Parties, gatherings, and celebrations
i. Occasional overnight guests (as in visiting friends from out of town)
j. Regular overnight guests (as in romantic partners)
k. Sharing the kitchen and pantry
l. Use of each other's personal property
m. Parking spaces
n. Thermostat and other utilities usage
o. What items or activities aren't allowed in the house

I cannot overstate the importance of negotiating clear expectations from the very onset of your relationship. You may not even be able to imagine some of the scenarios that might arise months down the road. For example, I included firearms as an item to discuss, because even though neither of you might own a gun, what if you're very much against having guns in your home and your roommate begins dating a person who carries a gun and brings it into the home? It's better to lay out the ground rules early on.

You may think that having friends over to hang out would be innocuous enough, but what happens when that "friend who never leaves" seems to be living on your couch? You may think that food costs can be split down the middle, but, again, what happens when you're paying for half the food but your roommate's "friend who never leaves" as well as her boyfriend are eating with you five nights a week?

When I was about 22, I moved to a new city, answered a classified ad, and moved in with a young woman who was about 19 and who seemed to be sweet and easy to get along with. She lived in a house her father owned, so she basically called the shots. We had no Roommate Agreement. After a few days, I discovered that she was dating a 40-year-old Hell's Angel who invaded our apartment with his pack of fellow riders and hung out for days, with heavy smoking and rowdy drinking, taking up all our shared space and leaving me almost in hiding in my bedroom. That was one of the few times I moved out rather than trying to negotiate a better relationship. I should've learned more about her before moving in. It was a lesson well learned!

Faith Fuson

Establishing Mutual Expectations for Shared Living

IN THIS CHAPTER, I address many practical issues. Use this section of the book as a guide for many of the items that you'll need to include in your Roommate Agreement when you move into a room or household with a new living partner.

Setting Up Your Agreed-Upon Expectations for Living Together

Arranging Your Space

So you've both moved into your shared space. This may be a dorm room, a suite, an apartment, or a house. It may have come already furnished with furniture, or both of you may be moving furniture into your place.

The first task of living together will be creating a comfortable and welcoming living space that's mutually agreeable and meets both of your needs (if you have more than one housemate, this process will need to expand to include the others, too).

Arranging the physical space may be easy if the place is already furnished. If it's not, then the interior design work kicks in! Let me warn you, however, that people tend to have strong feelings about where different pieces of furniture should go, so be prepared to use all your diplomatic skills (as well as to do a bit of rearranging to try different configurations of furniture layout for your public spaces).

If you find yourself at odds over where to put the sofa, for example, here are some tips for negotiating that'll help set the tone for a future amicable relationship. If your roommate asks why you want it on a particular wall, be sure to have some concrete, logical reasons you can share. Saying "Because I really like it there" gives your discussion no place to go and shuts it down. Saying "I like it there because the light comes in behind the sofa and won't be in my eyes" could be a good reason, or so could "If we put it in this position, we can see the television clearly." Be prepared with supporting reasons that make sense.

Be diplomatic, too. Let's say your roommate comes with the ugliest armchair you've ever seen. Instead of shouting, "Where did you get that monstrosity?", rein in your distaste and ask if they have an attachment to the chair (or perhaps its color or design). If they say, "Oh my god, yes! This is my favorite piece of furniture ever!", then you know you have little negotiating space if you want to make it disappear. If they say, "Oh, that's an old hand-me-down from my grandmother's cousin," you might suggest putting it either in an unobtrusive place or maybe covering it with a slipcover (which you can order online quite inexpensively) or even a blanket or quilt.

If your living area feels too crowded or cluttered because, between the two of you, you have too much stuff, you might suggest deciding together which pieces of furniture work best in the room and which ones might need to go somewhere else (either in one of the bedrooms or, um, elsewhere).

In the event that your roommate is more outspoken and controlling about needing to have everything arranged according to their plan, be sure to try to introduce a collaborative approach and stand up for your needs and desires as tactfully (but assertively) as possible.

Another problem you might encounter, especially if you're young and this is one of your first living situations away from your family home, is The Overbearing Parent Who Comes In And Takes Over. I've seen this happen more times than I'd like to remember. The roommate defers to their mother, a domineering would-be interior decorator who decides that her child can't possibly make decisions for themselves, and so she arranges the entire apartment while you are screaming internally.

Yes, I know it's really hard when you have people you barely know making decisions about your life! But remember—when the parents leave, you can sit down with the roommate and say, "Look, I know you appreciate your mom's help, and I know she meant well, but do you mind if we make some slight changes to the way she's set things up? For example, what about if we move this table over there and put the chair here instead? Would that work for you?"

In the end, decorating your shared living space should be a mutual decision that you and your roommate purposely make together. Be sure to avoid the passive-aggressive "moving things around when the roommate's out and hoping they won't notice" approach. Always agree upon it together.

Establishing Boundaries and Respecting Each Other's Privacy

Very early on, ideally in the first few days, you and your housemate should have a conversation about how each of you feels regarding what's private and what's public. Some of your living space will be shared, and some of it (in most cases) will be private for each of you.

Boundaries are extremely important, but they're also sometimes hard to talk about. More than just lines in the sand, they're emotionally loaded expectations attached to our sense of selfhood. Some of us grew up with strong, well-defined boundaries in our family lives, while some of us grew up in families where boundaries were never acknowledged. In the latter case, everything in a home was open to everyone, with little sense of private, personal space.

You can imagine what might happen when a person from each of those extremes moves in with one another. Tensions flare as the person expecting private, personal boundaries (let's say it's you) feels violated on a daily basis when the unknowing roommate walks into your bedroom uninvited, borrows your clothes or other possessions without asking, eats the food you've bought especially for yourself, or even reads your personal messages on your computer that you've left open.

On the other hand, the person from a low-boundaries family will wonder why you're so uptight, possessive, selfish, and rude about them just using what they perceived as stuff and space that is shared.

This is not a way to get off to a good start as housemates, so it's very important to discuss and delineate a mutually agreed upon arrangement of what the boundary expectations are for your household. Even better, you can write this into your Roommate Agreement.

The following are some things to consider as you discuss how to establish healthy boundaries in your first house meeting.

To Share or Not To Share Your Stuff?

This issue applies to everything from food to clothes, tools, and personal items. What will you share, and what's generally off-limits for each of you unless the other person specifically asks permission? In many households with kitchens, roommates will split grocery costs and agree upon certain food items that they'll share. They may also designate some food items as personal, only to be shared with permission. Nothing can be more disconcerting than buying a favorite food item, putting it in the fridge, and then coming home to find out that your roommate ate it all up.

Be sure to come to an agreement about which things are fine to share and which things need to be "yours" vs. "mine." You might make a list of basic stock items (oil, vinegar, mustard, ketchup, mayonnaise, salad dressing, flour, sugar, toilet paper, paper towels, napkins, etc.) that will be shared items, and create a budget for those so that you can estimate the monthly amount each of you will contribute. Of course, each of you will have your favorite foods that the other may not eat, so you won't share expenses on those. You might also want to have a place to keep a listing in case your roommate decides to share some of your foods (with your permission) so that they can pay you for their share of it, and vice versa. At the end of the month, you can reconcile to see how much you may owe each other.

It's always courteous to let your roommate sample some of the food you've bought, and vice versa, as long as they don't eat most of it. I had a roommate once who got mad because I used two of her mushrooms from a package of a dozen. If you're saving some food items for a special occasion, let the roommate know, but if you have a bottle of lemonade open in the fridge, don't be petty if your roommate would like a glass. Generally, partners who can give and take like that will get along much better and live together more happily.

Privacy vs. Togetherness

Boundaries are not just about physical space and the sharing of material possessions. They also involve understanding and setting expectations about how much of your personal time and space each of you feels comfortable doing things together as opposed to carrying on your separate lives and activities.

An example of a boundary misunderstanding here would be one roommate inviting a friend (or friends) over to eat dinner but not including the roommate, who feels left out and offended as a result. In that case, the one throwing the dinner party in the shared space should've informed the roommate ahead of time and asked if the roommate had any problems with using the shared space on that date. Out of courtesy, they might invite the roommate, especially if the roommate will be home that evening, but if it's a private dinner (let's say a date with a romantic partner), the one arranging the dinner should make that known as tactfully as possible to the roommate.

Another example would be when one roommate gets invited out to a party. Should the roommate expect the roommate to bring them along? This is where that boundary between roommate relationships and friendship comes in. One roommate shouldn't assume that the other is automatically going to be a "good friend," whether for hanging out together or for confiding in each other. While sometimes great friendships develop between roommates, don't go into the relationship expecting that will naturally be the case.

Emotional Boundaries

As mentioned elsewhere in this book, different personalities and those who come from different cultural and family backgrounds have quite distinct needs for "space" and alone time. This is clearly the case with extraverts as opposed to introverts in terms of personality types, but it's also related closely to those issues noted above regarding the way family cultures instill interpersonal boundary needs and the expectations that each person brings into the roommate situation.

This is an area that may need discussing repeatedly over a period of time as you and your living partner adjust to each other's needs for giving each other "space" and time alone and respecting the needs for separate lives. If you feel miffed because your housemate seems to ignore you and hardly ever speaks to you as they go about their own life, this doesn't necessarily mean that your roommate dislikes you or has a problem with you personally—it may well just reflect upon their need for privacy and space and their inclination to just live together amicably but not work on developing a friendship. This may be uncomfortable for you if your expectation is that roommates or housemates should hang out together and talk all the time. Get to know your roommate's expectations before you get upset and blow it up into a crisis.

One courtesy the two of you might agree upon is letting each other know when you're diverging from your normal schedule. This is a case in which your safety might become a concern if you suddenly seem to go missing. Of course, you may find a romantic partner and decide to spend a night or two at their place—but should you communicate that to your housemate? In my opinion, yes, you should. You can either tell them (if you know ahead of time) or text them that you won't be coming home that night. This is one case in which having someone to look out for your safety is worth involving that other person.

In the previous chapter, I mentioned physical touch, and this is definitely an issue that you and your roommate should address. Some of us are touchers and huggers, and some of us absolutely do not like being touched unless we invite it or agree to it. Just as you should do with all your friends and acquaintances, be sure to ask for consent the first few times you want to hug someone to find out how they feel about it. Once you've established a norm between the two of you, then everything should be fine. However, if either one of you feels tension about it, it's always good to revisit the conversation and ask if the other person is comfortable with your touch.

Studying or Working Remotely When You Share a Home

The guidance provided above about boundaries and respecting the other person's space also apply to situations in which either of you needs to study in your shared living space. If you're a person who can study while your roommate watches a movie or plays a video game, then sharing the living area won't be a problem. But keep in mind that it's a shared area that belongs to both of you, so if you're a person who needs absolute silence, then you should be the one to move into your private space, such as your bedroom, to study without distraction or interruption. Don't expect your roommate to be quiet or refrain from entertainment when you have another space in the house where you can study privately.

Similarly, if you or your roommate has a remote job working from home, it's the responsibility of whoever has the job to set up a private workspace area that won't preclude the roommate from using the public areas freely.

Cleanliness Tolerance in Shared Areas

There's a good possibility that you and your housemate may have different cleanliness standards, but remember: cleanliness can be measured in different ways. One has to do with literally keeping things clean and sanitary, such as wiping down counters, washing dirty dishes, keeping floors mopped or vacuumed, scrubbing toilets and showers to keep away grunge, and just keeping the house glistening clean in general.

Another difference in terms of cleanliness standards is tidiness versus clutter. A person can keep things clean by the above definition but still be disorganized and have their "stuff" piled everywhere. Instead of making sure everything "where it should be", a cluttered person has a high tolerance for letting the "stuff" find its own place wherever it may land—and stay there for as long as it wants to. Some people (me included) can feel perfectly comfortable living with stacks or piles of books, papers, or clothes.

However, as I know from much experience, the cluttered way of living can drive some housemates crazy. These housemates offended by clutter see disorder in all these piles and stacks, and they want everything returned to its rightful place.

Each of these philosophies is reasonable, and each is a perfectly fine way to live—except when you're living with someone whose expectations of cleanliness differ from yours. Some rules of thumb to ease this issue include discussing expectations for cleanliness in the common areas. How each person keeps their own private space is up to them. But compromise on both sides may be necessary if you have a clutterer and a tidier living together. In this case, each partner will need to move a bit toward the middle until you find a level in-between where each of you feels the least uncomfortable. It's usually the burden of the clutterer to make a bit more effort to either put things away or at least stack them neatly!

Dealing With Different Lifestyles and Schedules

In addition to all the other personality, family, and cultural differences we've covered thus far, there's another difference that can impact a roommate relationship, and it has to do with personal routines such as work and sleep schedules. Some of these are dictated externally and based on job hours or school hours. Some other differences may arise from each person's circadian rhythms.

Your circadian rhythm is your body's preference for when you go to sleep and when you wake up. Some of us may say we're a "morning person" or a "night owl" by nature. Whether due to our natural body clocks or the demands of our job schedules, each of us gets into routines regarding when we fall asleep and when we wake up. In addition, some people are nappers and need a bit of shut eye in the middle of the day.

If you and your housemate are on different sleeping and waking schedules, then each of you needs to be particularly considerate and respectful of the other's need for sleep. When you set up your Roommate Agreement and have your initial discussion, talk about these schedules and determine if and when you each need "quiet hours."

Pets

Whether you can have pets or not is probably determined by the terms of your rental agreement or rules regarding your housing community. If pets are allowed, that means that it's up to you and your roommate or housemate to agree upon whether having one or more pets will work in your shared space. It doesn't mean that any pet you get must have shared ownership, but, in most cases, a pet is one of those huge factors that cannot be kept privately in one person's room without affecting the life of the other person sharing the house or apartment. So for that reason, if either one of you desires a pet, you should get your housemate's approval.

Once you get a pet, the responsibility for who cares for the pet should be clear from the first moment it enters the home. Unless it's a shared pet with shared responsibilities, making sure that the animal gets proper and adequate food and water, exercise, veterinary care, and waste removal will be the owner's responsibility.

If you bring in a cat, for example, don't assume that your roommate will feed your pet or make sure the cat's litter box gets changed. And speaking of litter boxes (I should note that I'm a cat lover through and through), many a roommate relationship has ended because of inattention to these repositories of pet waste products. Your roommate may have a much more sensitive sense of smell than you do, and cat odors can be particularly noxious, so be sure to stay on your roommate's good side and keep the living space as fresh-smelling as possible!

If you do have a pet and you ever decide to go away for a few days or longer, remember that it's your responsibility to make arrangements for pet care while you're gone. Never just assume that your roommate will take care of it. Always communicate clearly.

Boyfriends, Girlfriends, and Guests (Especially Overnight Guests)

When you and a roommate are sharing a space, it's complicated enough just trying to work out ways for the two of you to live together harmoniously and in sync with each other's needs. When other people enter the equation, even for a short-term, their presence can throw things off balance. If one or both of you have friends or romantic partners who are spending significant time in your shared space, they become part of the equation—and sometimes, they create a need for the equation to be adjusted.

First, let me state that the two of you need an initial agreement about bringing friends to the house and about how long they can stay without becoming a burden (emotional or otherwise) to your roommate. This should be in your Roommate Agreement, and it will differ based on your personalities, so there's no hard-and-fast rule of guidance I can give. If one or both of you score high on the introvert scale, then your tolerance for having other people in your shared space will be much lower than if you're an extravert. Taking the Myers-Briggs personality type test (see Chapter 6 of this book) can help you both figure out what's reasonable.

Based upon my experience, having a friend come over for a meal or for an evening on occasion isn't an unreasonable expectation for either roommate, even introverts. However, if this occurs more than once or twice a week, then it can begin to become a burden to the roommate. Why? Consider this: the roommate and their friend(s) are likely using the public spaces, may be eating the shared food (in which case it becomes a financial issue as well), and imposing upon the goodwill and the right to privacy of the other roommate.

If this becomes a regular routine, then the two of you (without the friend or romantic partner) need to have a house meeting to discuss whether it's a tenable situation. Even if the roommate with the friend or lover stays sequestered in their bedroom, just the presence of another person in the house can rightfully make the other person feel uncomfortable and violate the original terms of just the two of you sharing a place together.

The issue of friends or romantic partners slowly "moving in" is a common one—and a serious one—that's often hard for the other housemate or roommate to deal with. The issue should be addressed as soon as it becomes clear that a third person is beginning to become a regular fixture in a two-person house. If the roommate with the partner intends for the cohabiting to become semi-permanent, then the two original housemates need to decide whether it would be best to continue in their current living arrangement or not. If they do decide to continue living together with the third person, then they'll need to establish new ground rules and new financial arrangements that are fair to the single housemate, then create a revised Roommate Agreement. If not, the couple may need to find a new living situation.

A different issue regarding guests involves visits by out-of-town friends or family members. In these cases, rather than assuming that having people crash in the house or apartment for a few days or a week is okay with the other roommate, always be courteous and ask. Be sure to realize that no matter where the guest or guests are staying, it'll be cramping your roommate's space, so do everything possible to extend every courtesy and consideration to your roommate.

Smoking, Drinking, and Other Substances

House rules about smoking, drinking, and drugs should be clear from the outset and written into the Roommate Agreement.

First and foremost, each roommate should commit to respecting the laws of your country, state, county, and/or municipal code. No roommate is expected to tolerate illegal activity in their own home, and, as such, any illegal activity is grounds for terminating the original agreement and contract.

Other guidelines become murkier and become mired in moral and health issues. Smoking is clearer, and many people who object to indoor smoke will state from the beginning that they want to live in a non-smoking household, an understanding which should be part of the Roommate Agreement and not violated. If one roommate smokes, even outdoors, and the scent lingers on their clothing, it can be physically repulsive to another person.

The question of drinking is more complicated. If the two of you are of legal drinking age, then you need to accept that drinking alcohol is a norm in mainstream American society. You or your roommate may have been raised in a non-drinking household, so either you might not drink or may not be accustomed to being around drinkers and the effects alcohol has on them. It may make you uncomfortable. If you've grown up in a family with an alcoholic parent, it may make you more than uncomfortable.

Moderate drinking, such as a beer or two in the evening or wine with dinner, is socially acceptable and shouldn't be a major concern. However, if you have a roommate who drinks excessively, gets drunk regularly, behaves erratically after drinking, or has other symptoms of alcoholism, you may have reason to want to leave the shared living relationship.

This is a tough emotional place to find yourself. Of course, you can suggest that your roommate get help if you believe they have a drinking problem, but, as a roommate, it's really not your job to try to fix the other person, so your decision will need to be whether you can tolerate the behavior or not.

Religious or Cultural Rituals

One of the most enlightening aspects of having roommates who come from religious or cultural backgrounds different from your own is that you have the opportunity to become exposed to new ways of living and seeing the world, as well as new cultural and religious practices.

In most cases, expressing a respectful curiosity about your roommate's practices will elicit an explanation to help you understand the basis of their culture or religion. This can be eye-opening!

It's very important not to be judgmental or self-righteous when dealing with people who do things differently from the way you were raised or what you believe. Try not to see a different perspective on life as a threat or a competition to your own way of living and worshiping. Instead, realize that people and cultures all over the world have found their own spiritual systems that provide support to them in their lives, and try to respect that.

Most of the time, your roommate's religious or cultural rituals shouldn't interfere with or impact your life all that much, especially if they are private or personal. However, in some cases, those beliefs and their associated practices will extend into your shared living space. In this case, you'll need to learn to respect and provide space for them.

Food Preparation, Eating, and Fasting

An example might be your roommate's cultural or religious rules for preparing food and eating. A code for eating, whether called kosher for members of the Jewish faith and tradition or halal for Muslims (those who follow Islam), may guide everything from the kinds of foods your roommate can eat to how they prepare it and even what dishes or implements they use for it. You may or may not eat with your roommate, but if you do, you'll need to learn to respect these codes.

Also, for Muslims, the holy month of Ramadan is a time when believers abstain from eating or drinking between dawn and sunset. If you have a Muslim housemate, be sure to respect their traditions during this time.

For Hindus and Buddhists, killing and eating living creatures is forbidden. Judaism and Islam both forbid their followers from eating pork, Orthodox Christians restrict meat intake on fasting days, and Catholics don't eat meat on Fridays.

Prayer and Holy Days

Prayer is another type of ritual that's common to many religions, but the way people pray and what times they pray vary a lot from religion to religion. Muslims honor a call to prayer (adhan) five times a day that involves performing a kneeling ritual (salah or salat) on a prayer rug. In Muslim communities, the adhan is broadcast as a musical chant from the rooftops of mosques.

Christians tend to pray together communally on their holy day or Sabbath, Sunday, when together in church. Many people, such as your potential Christian roommate, may have a private evening prayer ritual before bedtime and may also say a prayer before eating a meal.

If you have a Jewish roommate, they may celebrate Shabbat, which is the Jewish holy day or day of rest that begins at sunset on Fridays and continues until sunset on Saturdays. This usually involves a Shabbat dinner, with candles and special prayers. Services at the local synagogue may be on Friday evening or Saturday morning.

Managing Your Shared Living Space

When you and your housemate are establishing your Roommate Agreement, develop a list of household tasks that need to be done on a regular basis and determine who'll be responsible for each. These might be daily, weekly, or monthly chores, and you can either stay consistent with them or rotate them periodically. Below, a list of possible chores you might want to include:

Daily

- Meal preparation (if you cook and eat together)
- Cleaning dishes from the sink and loading the dishwasher
- Wiping down kitchen countertops
- Tidying up common areas and putting items in their proper places
- Unloading the dishwasher and putting away the dishes
- Taking out the trash when it's full

Weekly

- Vacuuming and/or sweeping the floors
- Dusting furniture surfaces and windowsills
- Cleaning out the refrigerator to get rid of old food
- Mowing the lawn
- Taking out the garbage for pickup
- Grocery shopping for food and household items
- Laundry (unless this is an individual responsibility)
- Scrubbing toilets and wiping bathroom counters
- Mopping the kitchen and bathroom floors

Monthly

- Cleaning kitchen cabinets inside and out
- Scrubbing out the refrigerator
- Thorough cleaning of kitchen counters (cleaning under and behind items on the countertop, stovetop, etc.)
- Reorganizing the pantry and cupboards in the kitchen
- Reorganizing closets, storage cupboards, and medicine cabinets
- Laundering the bathroom rug and other fabrics in house
- Tackling tough dirt on floors, walls, baseboards, and tile
- Checking the tub and shower for mold and mildew, scrubbing tile floors and walls
- Washing windows
- Dusting difficult-to-reach spots like light fixtures, ceiling fans, tops of high furniture, refrigerator, etc.

Managing Shared Finances

In addition to household chores, you'll need to assign responsibility for and reach agreements about how you'll be managing the household finances. If you share an apartment or house, you'll likely need an agreement about:

- paying rent
- splitting utility bills (electric, gas, water, phone, internet, garbage pickup, etc.)
- keeping financial records
- handling repair calls
- sharing and splitting costs for food, groceries, and household supplies

Set up a system for paying each other as promptly as possible. Platforms like Venmo or Zelle work well, as do PayPal transfers. Always keep records. Determine a schedule based upon when the rent or different utilities are due, and do your best to be financially responsible. Having to continually remind a roommate about overdue payments is difficult and can create tension in the relationship.

Faith Fuson

Establishing Healthy Patterns of Communication

YOU'RE ALL MOVED in, and now the task (and fun!) of relationship-building begins. Constructing a positive and respectful relationship with your roommate or housemate should start from Day One. How to go about it may feel different if you're both freshly moving in together to a new space than if one of you is moving into a place that the other has already been occupying, potentially replacing another housemate. You'll need to be sensitive to the dynamics if you're moving into an already-existing household. However, if you and a roommate are starting your household together from scratch, that provides many opportunities to work together to set up a system that functions well for both of you.

Even though said it was mentioned in the first chapter that your main role in a roommate relationship is not to necessarily try to become best friends with a roommate, the process of getting to know each other initially is not too different from friend-making.

The Steps in Developing a Roommate Relationship

Developing a strong roommate relationship generally involves several stages and steps, which may vary based on individual personalities and circumstances. However, some common elements of the process can include:

1. **Initial contact:** This stage involves the first meeting, whether it's a formal interview or just meeting someone casually through a friend and mentioning that you're looking for a roommate. This is when you assess each other and make first impressions, gaining some basic knowledge about the other person.
2. **Building rapport:** This stage may involve finding common ground, exchanging information about each other's interests, and engaging in conversations that lead to a greater understanding of one another.
3. **Spending time together:** As you build rapport, you'll typically need to spend some time together, whether it be hanging out, going to events, or engaging in mutual activities or interests. It may be working on a project at your shared home, such as redecorating a room or cooking a meal together.
4. **Sharing personal information:** As trust builds over time, the two of you may begin to share more personal information about yourselves, such as your feelings, goals, and struggles. However, this is not necessarily a requirement for roommates, as it leads into more of an emotional relationship than some roommates want, so it's perfectly fine if you don't want to make your roommate your confidante of BFF.
5. **Building a support system:** As relationships grow, roommates can often serve as a source of support for each other, helping each other out when need-

ed. For example, your housemate might offer to feed your cat while you're away for a weekend or to pick up some things for you at the supermarket while they are shopping.

6. **Long-term maintenance:** Maintaining roommate relationships involves nurturing them, which means never taking your roommate for granted, always being respectful, and continuing to learn what makes the other person tick and working to accommodate that whenever you can. The longer you live together, the better your understanding of each other, which will make you a great team.

The process of developing a roommate or housemate relationship is dynamic and everchanging. You may find that both of you put forth an initial burst of effort and energy, but then get caught up in your own lives and begin to neglect tending to your relationship. That can be a warning sign that you need to continue to focus and not start slacking on this important role that contributes to your comfortable and harmonious lifestyle.

How To Communicate Effectively With Your Roommate

Effective communication is the most essential skill in maintaining a positive relationship with your roommate. How do you communicate well?

First, *establish open communication* from the first day you move in together. Let your roommate know that you're open to discussing any issues or concerns, and encourage them to do the same. And do honor that pledge—if your roommate addresses a concern, don't shut down the conversation by becoming defensive or arguing. Be open, listen well, and don't take critiques as an attack.

Second, *listen actively*: Communication is a two-way street, so it's important to listen actively to your roommate's concerns. This means giving them your full attention, asking clarifying questions, and acknowledging their perspective. Let them know you heard them, then take some deep breaths before you respond to individual points. Use a calm tone instead of a confrontational one.

Third, *always be respectful* when communicating with your roommate, even if you disagree with them. Avoid using accusatory language or attacking them personally. Instead, focus on the issue at hand and how it can be resolved. Use "I" language instead of "you," which can come across as blaming (for example, use "I feel overwhelmed when the sink is full of dirty dishes" rather than "You always forget to wash the dishes").

Fourth, *be specific and avoid generalizing*. Try not to use words like "always" or "never," which can come across as accusatory and imply that the behavior is ongoing and unchangeable.

Fifth, *always address issues promptly*, and don't let them fester as the resentment and tension build up between you. This is a major problem when people fear conflict and confrontation, as their fear can create a passive-aggressive type of behavior. Be direct and timely.

Focus on finding solutions together. When working to resolve an issue with your roommate, try to find a solution that works for both of you. Ask your roommate for their suggestions, and brainstorm together to find creative solutions that address both of your needs.

After a conversation with your roommate, remember to follow up to doublecheck that the issue has been resolved and that both of you are satisfied with the outcome.

Remember, effective communication takes practice, so don't be discouraged if it takes some time to develop a positive communication dynamic with your roommate. Keep an open mind and be willing to work together to find solutions.

Holding House Meetings

When you live in a household, especially if there's more than two of you living together, holding more formal house meetings is an important way of setting aside dedicated time to talk in a businesslike way about any issues facing the household. You can hold house meetings even if there are just two of you as well, since it's important to create a distinct time and place for having serious conversations rather than just bringing up problems over a meal or while you're watching TV together, which can cause unnecessary tension.

Holding house meetings can be an effective way to discuss important topics, resolve conflicts, and make decisions with your housemates. Below, six tips on how to hold successful house meetings:

1. Schedule a time and place that works for all housemates. Make sure everyone is aware of the meeting time in advance, and give them plenty of notice.
2. Create an agenda beforehand that outlines the topics to be discussed during the meeting. This can help keep the conversation on track and ensure that all important issues are covered. Make sure everyone has input into building the agenda.
3. Encourage everyone to participate in the meeting by sharing their thoughts and opinions. Make sure everyone has an opportunity to speak and be heard.
4. Use respectful language during the meeting. Avoid making personal attacks or being defensive. Instead, focus on the issue and work together to find a solution.
5. Take notes to document the decisions. Assign someone to take notes during the meeting to record important action items. This ensures that everyone is on the same page and clearly understands what was discussed during the meeting.
6. Follow up with everyone after the meeting to make sure everyone is on board and working together toward a common goal.

By following these tips, you can hold successful house meetings that foster open communication and lead to positive outcomes.

Faith Fuson

About Personality Types

Understanding Personality Types

WE ALL LOVE those fun personality quizzes that come through our social media feeds. You've probably taken dozens of those little questionnaires on social media, the ones that reveal, "Which Harry Potter Character Are You?" or "Which Anime Personality Best Suits You and Your Lifestyle?" You've likely also heard warnings to avoid those quizzes, since their main purpose is to collect personal data about you so politicians or businesses can target you. (It's true.) And even though finding out the answer to "What Kind of Pizza Am I?" may be a silly distraction, you know deep down that those quizzes—or at least most of them—are not really valid and reliable ways to analyze your personality.

However, I can tell you about a personality test that really does have validity, rooted in scientific and psychological research—and it's not hocus pocus! The Myers-Briggs Type Indicator (MBTI) is a testing instrument that's been around since 1962.

Isabel Briggs Myers and her mother, Katherine Briggs, were fascinated by pioneering psychologist Carl Jung's theories of personality. Jung had published a book titled *Psychological Types: The Psychology of Individuation* in 1921. In his writing, Jung revealed that individuals experience the world in different ways, and he created a model, which Myers and Briggs refined, of our primary psychological functions. The Myers-Briggs assessment measures these in terms of how each of us gets our emotional energy, how we take in and process information, how we make decisions, and how we organize our world.

Carl Jung was first interested in the scale of *extraversion versus introversion*, believing that every person possesses the ability to be both extraverted and introverted. However, Jung also believed that one end of the spectrum tends to dominate a person's approach to interacting with the world and handling their own emotional energy.

He then distinguished two other scales: *intuition-sensation* and *thinking-feeling*, based on the same premise that, although each of us (1) approaches problem solving and knowledge-seeking both through our intuitive minds as well as our concrete, sensory experiences, and (2) approaches our interactions with and decisions about other people through both logical thinking and less-rational feeling, each of us tends to have a preference for one end of the scale or the other.

Finally, Jung also introduced what would be the fourth scale: *perception versus judgment*. I've always found these terms more difficult to explain than the concepts behind them. When you act upon *perception* in organizing your space or your time, you're making decisions that prioritize your personal experiences and impulses, while if you favor the opposite extreme, based upon *judgment*, you rely heavily upon society's rules and structures to guide you.

So the mother-daughter team of Myers and Briggs further developed Jung's concepts of types, using the four scales to create an easily understood model:

Extraversion (E) ß ---------------- | ---------------- à Introversion (I)

Sensing (S) ß ---------------------- | ------------------ à Intuition (N)

Thinking (T) ß -------------------- | -------------------- à Feeling (F)

Judging (J) ß ---------------------- | ---------------- à Perceiving (P)

Taking the Myers-Briggs Type Indicator Assessment

Through a test that consists of answering a series of seemingly simple questions about your own personal preferences, the MBTI assessment will place you on each scale. Although it's possible to fall right in the middle of one or more of the scales, most people show a distinct preference and land on one side or the other. Where you land on the scale indicates the strength of your position, so, for example, you can be mildly extraverted or strongly extraverted. In both cases, the test would classify you as E, but knowing the strength of that degree of extraversion will help you in your self-interpretation.

As you can see, if each person's testing places them along each of the four scales, they'll end up with a four-letter code for their MBTI personality type. With four scales, we end up with 16 possible combinations, so in the following sections, we'll go over each of these 16 MBTI personality types in relationship to sharing a living space.

The MBTI has become a useful tool to help people become more self-aware and to better understand others in their lives and relationships. Personality testing is widely used in the business world and within nonprofit organizations to help with career counseling, team building, and job placements. Knowing your personality type can provide insights into the best types of careers and working conditions that match your preferences and abilities. MBTI trainers and consultants also frequently use the assessment to help workplace teams learn to work together more productively and to overcome conflict.

Similarly, understanding MBTI personality types is also extremely helpful in negotiating relationships, from romantic couples to friendships to roommates. Whether you get tested formally as part of a workshop or you choose to self-test and learn about interpreting the results on your own, what you learn about yourself from the MBTI assessment will be useful to you throughout your life.

If you're a college or university student, your university's career or counseling office will likely be able to administer the test and help you interpret it to learn more about yourself. I invite you to stop and take a moment and discover your personality type. Ask your roommate to complete this with

Scan QR Code for Free 16 Personalities Test

you and have some fun with it. Discover the true essence of your personality and gain invaluable insights into your strengths, weaknesses, and unique qualities by taking the free 16 Personalities test.

Uncover a deeper understanding of yourself, your interactions with the world, and how others perceive you, paving the way for personal growth and self-awareness. The site also provides information about each of the 16 different personality types, with information about strengths and weaknesses, careers, and relationships for each. You can also find many published books, as well as information from various sites that will tell you more about your personality type.

Please keep in mind one important fact. *Your assigned type is based on your responses to the test questions.* It's very important that when taking the test, you're extremely honest about your preferences. Don't give the answer that you think is the most socially acceptable or the answer that reflects the way your parents raised you—unless it truly reflects your deepest preferences. *Being honest and self-aware is essential if you want an accurate result.* Also, remember that you may score closer to the center line on one or more scales and, if so, you may find yourself in between two types. For example, if you're right on the line between sensing (S) and intuition (N), but score more definitively on the other scales as E, F, and P, you may find that information on both ESFP and ENFP types is relevant to you.

Now, let's turn to the question of how your MBTI personality type and that of your potential housemate or roommate can help you understand how well you might (or might not) live together. Keep in mind that it always takes two to create a successful relationship, so the whole purpose of this book is to help you learn to negotiate a positive working relationship with at least one other person.

Living With People Whose Preferences Are Different From Yours

Optimal roommate relationships don't just naturally occur—they take a willingness to work out the tangles that you'll invariably encounter along the way. I hope this section opens your eyes to all the positive qualities that each of you can contribute to your roommate relationship.

You may wonder: when you're looking for a roommate, should you find a clone of yourself or someone who's a total opposite? Actually, neither one is necessarily a bad idea, depending upon whether you'd prefer to live with someone who looks at the world the same way you do (but who may also have tendencies to fall into the same bad habits as you) or to live with someone whose traits can balance and complement yours in some areas.

The E-I Scale

If you're mildly introverted, you might prefer to live with someone who's a bit more sociable and extraverted than you are but who'll also respect your needs for quiet time by yourself and in your own space. Housemates who are extremes on either end of the scale will probably drive each other crazy, since the E roommate will be much needier for companionship, while the I roommate will feel like they never have a moment alone.

If you're an E, don't take it personally when your introverted housemate goes into their room and closes the door. That's what an introvert needs to recharge their batteries. It doesn't mean they don't like you or that they're unfriendly. And if you have an introverted (I) personality, try to dedicate spending some structured time each week to satisfying your E roommate's need for company and hanging out together, but then diplomatically assert your boundaries.

Introverts also prefer one-to-one relationships to groups, so partying with crowds often turns them off or emotionally drains them. That doesn't mean they're not sociable; instead, they enjoy interacting with just one or two people at a time.

The S-N Scale

Sensors (S) and intuitives (N) come with different ways of thinking and processing information. Intuitives tend to live more in the world of their minds and can abstractly imagine the outcomes of decisions, while their sensory roommates need hands-on, physical, experiential evidence to draw the connections between the dots. Neither is smarter than the other: they just process information differently. Another way to look at the difference between the two types is that an N tends to look at the big picture first—the forest, if you will—while their S counterpart will focus their attention on the details—or the trees—first.

How might that affect you when living together? This difference can lead to disagreements about how to work on a project together, whether it's a housecleaning job or planning a dinner party. These different preferences will lead each of you to approach the task from a distinct angle. Let's say you plan to cook a meal together. If you're an S, you're probably a person who follows a recipe step-by-step and measures ingredients exactly (especially if you're an SJ). At the least, you'll start by focusing on the small details.

On the other hand, your N (and especially NP) roommate may be more of an improvisational cook who might glance at the recipe but then set the book aside and throw in "a little of this and a little of that"—and even make a few substitutions. Neither way is wrong or right, but it's the getting there that's different. It can cause conflicts when planning until you each recognize the strengths of the other's preferences.

The T-F Scale

Now, the thinking-feeling scale is one where housemates with opposing types need to really work to learn to understand each other. You might think of it this way: a thinker (T) leads with their rational mind and makes decision based upon rules, while a feeler (F) leads with their heart and may disregard rules to consider emotional concerns. Making decisions together is hard if each of you is working from a different set of criteria about how to evaluate a situation.

Let's say you have a disagreement because a third housemate did something to violate your house rules.

The thinker (T) housemate is more likely to consider what is fair and just, based on logic and society's norms (as well as any written guidelines). The feeler (F) roommate is more likely to look at each individual situation and make allowances for extenuating circumstances, letting their sympathy guide them to, say, give the other person another chance or not judge them so harshly.

The J-P Scale

From my experience, this scale is at the heart of most roommate disagreements, since it can cause the most conflicts. Judgers (J) tend to want to *impose order on their environment* as well as to *structure their time* with precision. Perceivers (P) are more likely to be less structured, so they can tolerate more clutter or lack of organization around the living space. They may also be much "looser" in terms of scheduling their time, wanting to allow for more spontaneity. They may not use a planner to make appointments and plan agendas but instead wait to see what they feel like doing each day.

You can see where this might lead from Day One with opposing roommates! Neither is better; they just bring different approaches to organizing their space and/or time.

If you're living with an opposite on this scale, then you need a mutually agreed-upon strategy that allows you both to live in the same space without having a daily argument. Often, an agreement to keep shared spaces tidy, while allowing for a "to each their own" philosophy in private spaces, will work. Another tactic is to divide the cleaning chores so that each person gets to take care of the tasks that they care most about. In the end, compromise rules! The J roommate may need to learn to tolerate a bit more disorder, while the P roommate may need to make a more purposeful effort to do their share.

Faith Fuson

The Myers-Briggs Personality Types as Roommates

IN THIS CHAPTER, let's look at each of the 16 Myers-Briggs personality types. Here, we'll focus on two questions about each type: in what ways does each MBTI personality type make good roommates or housemates? And, conversely, what are some potentially irritating habits each type of roommate might have?

Whether you're in the preliminary stages of thinking about what kind of roommate or housemate you'd like to live with, or you already have a living partner and need to learn how to understand each other so that you can live together optimally, the following nuggets of information about each MBTI type can help you. While this chapter is about living with roommates with various character traits and lifestyle preferences, the next chapter will be about examining yourself and your own personality type. Both chapters together will assist you in developing a better understanding of how people with different personalities can live together happily despite any differences in styles, habits, and temperaments.

ENTJ: "The House Manager"

The Upside

Are you looking for a likeable roommate who's fun to hang around with but who'll stay on top of tasks and get things done? ENTJs can make great housemates because they tend to be:

1. **Proactive problem solvers:** They can quickly identify problems and develop practical solutions. This trait can be especially helpful when it comes to addressing household issues or conflicts.

2. **Organized and efficient:** ENTJs are often extremely efficient at managing household tasks and schedules. As housemates, they may be good at ensuring that everyone in the household is contributing to the upkeep of the living space.

3. **Clear communicators:** They're typically direct and assertive, which can help prevent misunderstandings and ensure that everyone is on the same page. Also, they may take leadership in establishing clear rules and expectations for living together.

4. **Goal oriented:** Their focus on achieving their personal goals might inspire and motivate you and other housemates to stay on track with your own goals and responsibilities.

5. **Social and outgoing:** ENTJs tend to be sociable, which can make them good at building a sense of community among housemates, as they foster a positive and supportive living environment.

6. **Decisive:** They're known for their ability to make tough decisions quickly. An added bonus of living with an ENTJ is that they can help you make decisions and provide you with guidance and support.

7. **Driven:** Highly motivated, ENTJs are always looking for ways to improve themselves and their surroundings.

The Downside

While ENTJs can be great housemates, they—just like everyone else—bring their own set of quirks that may be irritating at times, especially to housemates with different personality types. Below, we'll examine some potentially annoying habits that an ENTJ housemate may have.

ENTJs can be very assertive and have strong opinions, which is great in a leadership role, but this may come across as overbearing to others. Some ENTJs have a tendency to micromanage and take control of household decisions. Also, while focused on achieving their goals, they may seem to lack empathy in terms of considering the feelings of those they live with. Their T (thinking) and J (judging) combination may make them seem cold, distant, or insensitive at times, especially if you're a feeler (F) and/or perceiver (P).

Especially if you're a perceiver (P), your ENTJ roommate may seem impatient, as ENTJs are often in a hurry to get things done and can get exasperated with others who don't move at their pace or do things on their schedule. Similarly, you might perceive your ENTJ housemate as being inflexible if they seem to have a rigid approach to household routines and schedules.

ENTJs can also be very critical of themselves and others. They often hold high standards and expectations, and they can be quick to point out flaws or mistakes in their housemates' behavior or work. Don't take it personally—they can be as hard on themselves as they are on others!

If you live with an ENTJ and experience any of these frustrations, the best strategy is to try to understand each other's personality preferences and work to find a mutually agreeable style of living and interacting that suits both your needs and those of your roommate's. Communication is the key!

ENTP: "The Easygoing Problem Solver"

The Upside

Do you want a housemate who takes things in stride without stressing too much? An ENTP can be fun to have around and will always keep life interesting. This personality type can be a super housemate for several reasons. They may be:

1. **Creative and energetic:** ENTPs are known for their ability to come up with innovative solutions to problems and finding creative ways to address household issues or conflicts. Their creative and innovative energy can contribute to an exciting and dynamic home environment. When you're looking for someone to brainstorm fun and inventive ideas for activities or ways to improve the living space, find an ENTP!

2. **Flexible and adaptable:** These qualities can help ENTPs accommodate the needs and preferences of their housemates.
3. **Sociable and outgoing:** An ENTP's social skills can enhance their ability to build connections with their housemates and organize social events or gatherings.
4. **Good at brainstorming:** ENTPs excel at generating ideas for planning household activities, decorating, or solving problems together.
5. **Playful and lighthearted:** Their often playful and lighthearted approach to life can help create a fun and relaxed living environment. They're generally great at making their housemates laugh and bringing a sense of humor to the household.
6. **Intellectually stimulating:** ENTPs enjoy learning and exploring new ideas, which can make for stimulating conversations and discussions. They may challenge their housemates to think critically and expand their knowledge.

The Downside

ENTPs make wonderful housemates and offer a distinctive personality to the household, but like all of us, each ENTP roommate can have personality traits that might irritate their roommates, especially those of an opposite personality type.

If you're an orderly and structured person (likely a J for judging), then you may perceive your living partner as slightly disorganized. This trait can show itself in terms of how they arrange and take care of their space, which may seem messy, and you might feel resentful if they forget to clean up after themselves in your shared areas.

In terms of time and planning, ENTPs tend to be very flexible and spontaneous, so they may not be as methodical and schedule-oriented as some housemates would like them to be. This may seem irresponsible and impulsive if you're an opposite type (a J).

One trait related to perceivers (P) can be procrastination, and ENTPs can get easily distracted by new ideas—they may put off doing tasks they find boring or uninteresting. They can be very enthusiastic about new ideas and projects, but they may not always follow through on them. This tendency for distraction can also make them seem inattentive or disinterested when they're with you. It's not unusual for ENTP housemates to get caught up in their own thoughts and projects and not always be fully present in the moment when you need their attention.

The thinking (T) side of ENTPs may make them seem argumentative, especially if you're a feeler (F). This personality type enjoys debating, and may come across as confrontational or insensitive if they push too hard on certain issues.

One great quality about this personality type is that your ENTP housemate will likely be open to communicating clearly with you as the two of you sit down and express your needs and preferences. Doing so will help the two of you find a common ground that enables you to live together in harmony.

INTJ: "The Respectful Organizer"

The Upside

Do you get along well with people who respect your boundaries? An INTJ roommate may be a good match because they're likely to be:

1. **Respectful of personal space:** INTJs typically value their own personal space and privacy, which can make them considerate and respectful housemates. They tend to be mindful of their housemates' need for space and quiet time.

2. **Organized and efficient:** They can be highly organized and efficient, making them effective at managing household tasks and schedules. Your INTJ housemate may take the lead at keeping the living space clean and tidy and ensuring that everyone shares household responsibilities fairly.

3. **Good at problem solving:** INTJs are often skilled problem solvers and may be good at finding creative solutions to household issues or conflicts. If you need help identifying the root cause of problems and developing practical solutions, lean on your INTJ housemate.

4. **Clear communicators:** They're typically straightforward and direct communicators, which can help avoid misunderstandings and conflicts common with housemates. You can expect them to express their needs and expectations clearly and to listen actively to others.

5. **Respectful of rules and boundaries:** INTJs tend to be rule followers, and so they may be adept

at adhering to established household rules and boundaries. They'll likely also want to enforce rules fairly and impartially.

The Downside

INTJs make awesome housemates, but if you have opposing personality types on one or more of the MBTI scales, living with an INTJ may take some getting used to. Some potentially irritating habits that an INTJ housemate might have include aloofness, perfectionism, lack of flexibility, bluntness, and workaholism.

INTJs can be very private, and they may not be as outgoing or sociable as extraverted (E) and/or feeling (F) roommates would like them to be. They might prefer to spend their time alone or working on their own projects, which can make them seem distant or detached. Housemates with this personality type can also be very direct and may not always consider the feelings of others when they speak their minds, coming across as insensitive or tactless if they don't filter their words carefully.

INTJs tend to have high standards and expectations, so they might get frustrated if you don't share their attention to detail or work ethic. If things aren't done to their satisfaction, they may come across as critical or nitpicky. Your INTJ roommate may also have a more rigid approach to household routines and schedules than you do.

With a tendency to hyperfocus on their goals, like studying or working, INTJs can be very driven and, in some cases, may neglect their household duties or social obligations. They may seem distant or detached from their housemates if they spend too much time working or pursuing their personal interests.

The solution to any of these perceived problems between you and your INTJ roommate is to sit down and clearly communicate with one another as you grow to understand each other's personalities and needs.

INTP: "The Adaptable Peacemaker"

The Upside

If you need a flexible, easygoing roommate who's always interesting to talk to, try living with an INTP! They tend to be:

1. **Independent:** INTPs typically value their own personal space and time. They're generally good at respecting the personal space and privacy of their housemates and allowing them the freedom to do their own thing.

2. **Creative problem solvers:** They're known for their ability to analyze complex problems and come up with creative solutions. This can be helpful when it comes to addressing household issues or conflicts.

3. **Open-minded:** Curious about the world around them, INTPs are usually fairly tolerant at accepting different lifestyles and perspectives, making them flexible housemates.

4. **Good at brainstorming:** INTPs are often creative at generating ideas, which can be beneficial when it comes to planning household activities

or finding solutions to problems together with their housemates.

5. **Easygoing and flexible:** Their laidback and easygoing approach to life can help create a relaxed and stress-free living environment. INTPs can also be quite good at diffusing tensions and maintaining a positive atmosphere in your home. They can be flexible and adaptable, making them good at adjusting to changing living situations and accommodating the needs and preferences of their housemates.

6. **Intellectually stimulating:** INTPs tend to be intellectually curious and enjoy discussing complex ideas and theories. Living with an INTP can provide an opportunity for engaging conversations and debates, which can be intellectually stimulating.

The Downside

As much as you may love living with your INTP roommate, some of their personality traits may drive you bonkers if you're extraverted, extremely well-organized, and easily annoyed. People with the INTP personality type who are extreme introverts (I) tend to pull into their own shells, socially withdrawing to spend time alone and pursue their own interests. This isn't because they don't like you; they just need their own space.

Because they tend to be focused on their own thoughts and ideas, an INTP housemate doesn't always prioritize keeping their living space neat and tidy. They can also be absent-minded and forget to do things, like household chores or social obligations, that you're relying on them to do.

One of the characteristics of intuitive perceivers (NPs) is that they enjoy considering all the possibilities and may struggle to make decisions quickly, which can be frustrating for more decisive housemates. This also relates to a tendency for procrastination. "I'll do it when I get around to it" can be a typical answer to a preoccupied INTP roommate, but that response can feel infuriating to you if you value honoring a time schedule and commitments. If you live with an INTP, it's important to communicate openly about your concerns and find ways to work together effectively as housemates.

ENFJ: "The Compassionate Social Manager"

The Upside

Would you like a warm, empathetic, and organized housemate? When you live with an ENFJ, they can:

1. **Foster a positive and harmonious living environment:** ENFJs are often skilled at creating a warm and welcoming atmosphere, which can be valuable in a housemate situation. They may prioritize creating a harmonious living environment, whether it's by arranging shared spaces in a thoughtful manner, organizing social events with other housemates, or simply being a supportive and caring presence in the home.

2. **Be considerate, supportive, and empathetic:** They tend to be highly empathetic, which can be a valuable trait in a housemate. Often attuned to

your needs and emotions, these housemates may go out of their way to be considerate and supportive. They can be wonderful housemates to turn to when you need emotional support or a listening ear during a tough time.

3. **Be organized and responsible:** ENFJs often take on a leadership role in organizing household tasks and responsibilities or keeping shared spaces clean and tidy.

4. **Radiate positive energy:** They tend to have an enthusiastic energy that can be infectious and uplifting. ENFJs may bring a sense of optimism and enthusiasm to shared experiences and social events, helping to create a fun and engaging atmosphere.

5. **Help resolve conflicts:** ENFJs tend to be skilled at navigating interpersonal conflict and mediating difficult situations in a constructive and productive way. They may look for solutions that work for everyone involved to help defuse tense situations before they escalate.

The Downside

While ENFJ roommates can be perfectly delightful companions, they may also have some habits that could be irritating to you depending upon your own personality type. ENFJs tend to be highly emotional and empathetic individuals, which can be a positive quality but can also be overwhelming for some housemates. Their intense emotions may be difficult to handle, especially if they're going through a difficult time.

ENFJs value harmony and sometimes avoid conflict at all costs. While this can be a positive trait, it can also mean that failing to address issues or concerns between members of the household can lead to simmering tensions or unresolved problems. Also, as people pleasers, ENFJ housemates may neglect their own needs and boundaries. This can be frustrating for you as a housemate if you feel responsible for always looking out for your roommate's needs.

On the flip side, some ENFJs tend to take charge and make decisions for others, which can come across as overbearing or controlling. They tend to be very busy people, often involved in many different activities and social circles. While this is an attractive quality, it can also mean that you may not see your social butterfly roommate as much as you might like. Communication and compromise can help ensure a positive and harmonious living situation for all.

ENFP: "The Enthusiastic Motivator"

The Upside

How about a roommate who's full of positive energy and who communicates well? Living with an ENFP can be an exciting and enriching experience, as they may be:

1. **Creative and adventurous:** ENFPs can bring a sense of fun and excitement to the home. Eager to enjoy trying new activities and experiences, they may also be creative in coming up with ways to decorate or organize shared spaces.

2. **Social and outgoing, with positive energy:** These qualities make ENFPs perfect for building connections and relationships with other housemates. Their enthusiastic energy can be infectious and uplifting in a living situation. They may enjoy going out and exploring new places, or they may be handy at organizing pleasurable and engaging activities at home. Many ENFPs flourish when hosting social events and bringing people together, which can be an excellent way to build community and foster connections with other housemates.

3. **Flexible and adaptable:** An ENFP housemate is usually easy to live with. They may be open to new ideas and ways of doing things, and they can adjust to different schedules or living arrangements.

4. **Empathetic and supportive:** They're typically valuable listeners and confidantes. They may be able to offer emotional support and guidance when you need it.

5. **Great communicators:** ENFPs are likely to not be shy about expressing their needs and concerns clearly. They may be able to help mediate conflicts or misunderstandings in a constructive way.

The Downside

ENFP roommates can energize your living situation with fun and creativity. However, as with any personality type, you'll find times when their behaviors and styles can rub you the wrong way, especially if you have some opposite preferences.

A potentially annoying habit of an ENFP roommate might be keeping disorganized living spaces, which may feel chaotic and uncomfortable if you're an extremely orderly person. They may leave their stuff lying around and forget to wash the dishes or wipe the counters.

Because they prefer to be spontaneous and impulsive—catching life's experiences as they happen rather than planning them in advance—you might feel frustrated if your ENFP housemate has trouble sticking to plans or commitments. They often change their minds at the last minute or choose a more appealing option that pops up.

Related to this, you might feel that your ENFP housemate is irresponsible about following through on commitments and plans. They sometimes enthusiastically start new projects and get excited about new ideas but fail to see them through to completion.

ENFPs can be extremely social and thrive being around a lot of people, which can present a problem if you're an introvert (I) and your ENFP housemate brings a lot of friends home to hang out. Also, some ENFPs can get highly emotional and can be prone to mood swings or emotional outbursts. This can be difficult for roommates to handle, especially if you feel like you're walking on eggshells around them.

If you experience any of these issues, learning to communicate clearly with your housemate and setting mutual expectations is an important step in living with an ENFP.

INFJ: "The Empathetic Mediator"

The Upside

If you feel good about having a roommate who won't crowd you but is reliable, insightful, and respectful, you may find what you need with an INFJ. An INFJ housemate can be:

1. **Deeply empathetic and understanding:** INFJs are often highly attuned to the feelings and needs of others, which can make them superb housemates to turn to when you need emotional support or a listening ear. They may be able to offer insightful advice or a fresh perspective on difficult situations.

2. **Insightful and intuitive:** They can be quite perceptive at understanding people and situations on a deep level, thanks to their intuition and ability to relate to people. They're often able to read between the lines and pick up on subtleties that others miss, which can be helpful in a living situation.

3. **Responsible and reliable:** You can usually count on INFJs to keep shared spaces clean and tidy and to pay their share of the bills on time.

4. **Independent and respectful:** INFJs tend to value their independent space are generally respectful of your boundaries and needs as well. Even when they prioritize personal space, they can also build strong and meaningful connections with their roommates.

5. **Good at conflict resolution:** They tend to be skilled at navigating interpersonal conflict, and

they're usually quite adept at mediating difficult situations in a constructive and productive way. They might look for solutions that work for everyone involved to help resolve tense situations.

The Downside

INFJs usually make quite kind and thoughtful roommates, but depending upon your own personality type, you might find some of their habits and behaviors aggravating from time to time. Since INFJs are introverted, they may need a lot of alone time to recharge their batteries. Their need for privacy can be difficult if you enjoy socializing or feel like your INFJ roommate is isolating themselves.

As intuitives, INFJs are prone to overthinking, and they may spend a lot of time analyzing and processing their thoughts and emotions. Often idealistic, they have high expectations for themselves and others. They can also be perfectionists who have high standards for their living space. These characteristics might lead you to feel like your INFJ roommate is judging you for not meeting their standards. Remember not to take it personally—they're hard on themselves, too!

Being highly empathetic, your INFJ housemate may be prone to intense emotions, which you might find overwhelming. However, be sure to set boundaries and communicate clearly and compassionately about how you're feeling to let your roommate know when you feel uncomfortable. Using your emotional intelligence to establish a mutually open and honest relationship can make all the difference and help you avoid a personality clash.

INFP: "The Considerate Collaborator"

The Upside

Another wonderful roommate choice can be an INFP. With this personality type, you'll get a thoughtful and empathetic living partner full of creative energy. Some qualities you might find are:

1. **Empathy and understanding:** INFPs tend to be deeply attuned to other peoples' feelings and needs, so they often provide excellent emotional support and feedback. This could include things like helping you out when you need it, cooking meals, or simply being there to listen when you need to talk.

2. **Creativity and imagination:** They're often creative and imaginative, which can make them fabulous partners to collaborate with on decorating or organizing shared spaces. They may have inspiring ideas for creating a comfortable and welcoming home environment.

3. **Idealism and values:** When you find an INFP, you'll often find strong values and a desire to make the world a better place. They're excellent partners on shared projects or volunteer initiatives who may inspire you to think more deeply about your own values and goals.

4. **Respectful and considerate:** Tending to be respectful of your needs and boundaries, INFPs may contribute greatly to creating a peaceful and har-

monious living environment. Skilled at negotiating shared spaces and responsibilities, this housemate is often able to foster compromise to ensure that everyone feels comfortable and respected.

5. **Introspective insights:** INFPs are often reflective about their own thoughts and feelings, making excellent housemates with whom to work through difficult issues or conflicts. As well, they may be able to offer unique and thoughtful perspectives on difficult situations as they help you or others to process emotions.

The Downside

Although you may feel a strong connection to your INFP roommate's distinctive personality, you may also get tired of some of their habits and dispositions. An INFP roommate who focuses on their inner thoughts and ideas more than the space around them can seem messy if you tend to prefer structure, order, and cleanliness in your living environment.

Interpersonally, INFPs are known for their aversion to conflict. They may either avoid addressing issues or disagreements with you or other housemates or get awkward when trying to address them. This might make you feel like your roommate isn't hearing your concerns. Similarly, INFPs can be highly sensitive, and they often take criticism or negative feedback personally. This can be challenging if you need to communicate constructive criticism or feedback in a direct and honest way.

INFP housemates may prefer spontaneous decision making rather than long-term appointment setting. This can make them seem impulsive, but when the moment feels right to them, they want to seize it. On the other hand, their habit of procrastinating might make you feel like time doesn't matter to them—and in many cases, deadlines aren't as important to an INFP as what they're involved in at any given moment.

Knowing their tendency to avoid conflict, it's always best to approach any communication about improving your roommate relationship with lots of reassurance and in a friendly way rather than in a blaming manner that will make them defensive. Once they feel safe, you'll likely be able to communicate well and work out a plan to find common ground for harmonious living.

ESTJ: "The Structured Goal-Setter"

The Upside

If you're looking for a housemate who'll help get the place organized, an ESTJ can be a reliable, take-charge kind of housemate. Some of the best qualities an ESTJ roommate tends to have are:

1. **Efficient and organized:** This personality type is known to be orderly and disciplined, which can make them ideal housemates if you value structure and routine. ESTJ roommates are often able to help keep shared spaces clean and tidy, and they're likely skilled at managing household tasks and responsibilities.

2. **Responsible and reliable:** ESTJs tend to be responsible and reliable, which means you can

count on them for tasks or commitments and for following through on their promises. They may be willing to take on additional responsibilities to ensure that the household runs smoothly.

3. **Assertive and decisive:** Many impressive leaders and problem solvers share this personality type. They may be able to take charge in difficult situations, mediate conflicts, or make tough decisions.

4. **Goal-oriented and focused:** ESTJs are usually delightful housemates to work with on shared projects or initiatives. They can provide a clear direction and structure for group efforts, keeping everyone on-track and motivated.

5. **Honest and direct:** They tend to be honest and direct in their communication, which will win you over if you value clarity and transparency. They may be able to provide constructive feedback or criticism in a straightforward and respectful manner.

The Downside

The efficient ESTJ housemate can be a wonderful companion, especially if you have similar or complementary styles. However, a few aspects of the ESTJ personality may feel off-putting if you aren't used to this "take charge" personality type.

When it comes to doing things a particular way, the ESTJ self-confidence may come across as controlling to roommates. ESTJs often have strong opinions on how things should be done and may not be as open to compromise or different perspectives as other personality types. They value structure and order, but their routines or expectations might feel rigid and frustrating to you, especially if you prefer a less-structured (or differently structured) approach.

Interpersonally, ESTJs can be very direct and may not always consider how their words or actions might affect others. You may feel like your housemate is bossy because they prioritize efficiency over feelings, which can be challenging for roommates who value emotional intelligence and sensitivity. Similarly, their focus on results may make them impatient or frustrated when things don't go their way.

ESTJs are often very dedicated to their work and can prioritize it above socializing or spending time with roommates. They may also bring work-related stress or concerns into your shared living space, which can be draining for roommates to deal with.

ESTP: "The Fun-Loving Companion"

The Upside

Living with an ESTP can be a dynamic and exciting experience, as they're known for their outgoing, energetic, and adventurous personalities. The following are some qualities of ESTPs that you might enjoy:

1. **Fun and adventurous**: ESTPs tend to be fun-loving and open to new experiences, which can make them energizing housemates if you value excitement. They're often terrific at planning social activities or outings, generally always willing to try new things and explore new places.

2. **Confident and assertive:** Usually self-assured and clear in their communication, this personality type can thrive as leaders and problem solvers. They usually handle difficult situations well, and they often face conflicts and make tough decisions with skill.

3. **Energetic and active:** Many ESTPs tend to be full of energy, which can be invigorating if you value physical fitness, sports, and outdoor activities. Talented at encouraging others to exercise or participate in sports, they'll often be eager to organize group activities or events.

4. **Resourceful and adaptable:** Able to offer creative solutions to household problems or tasks, ESTPs usually find ways to make the most of limited resources.

5. **Charismatic and sociable:** The outgoing and people-loving ESTP type makes a wonderful roommate if you like socializing and building relationships. Experts at networking or connecting with others, they're often known for bringing a lively energy to the household.

The Downside

Your spontaneous, action-oriented ESTP roommate can bring a lot of excitement into your life, but some parts of their personality might start aggravating you after a while. That same impulsiveness and risk-taking that makes them so much fun to do things with can also lead to unexpected or disruptive behavior.

They may decide to have a party or bring home a new pet or love interest without consulting their roommates, which can be frustrating if you value structure and predictability. Their thrill-seeking can also lead to dangerous or disruptive behavior that affects not only them but also others in the living space.

ESTPs may sometimes prioritize having fun over taking care of responsibilities, such as paying bills or cleaning up after themselves. This can be frustrating for housemates who value reliability and accountability. ESTPs can also sometimes struggle with organizing their living space as well as with schedules or routines, which can be frustrating to highly organized housemates.

At an interpersonal level, ESTPs can sometimes be blunt and straightforward, not realizing how their words or actions might affect others. You might think they lack emotional sensitivity or empathy, so it can be easy to have your feelings hurt.

ISTJ: "The Reliable Organizer"

The Upside

Do you value living with a dependable person that you can count on to respect rules and traditions? As housemates, ISTJs are known for their practicality and attention to detail. Some of the best features of living with an ISTJ include their ability to be:

1. **Reliable and consistent:** If you value dependability and predictability, choose an ISTJ roommate.

They often excel at following through on commitments and keeping a consistent schedule.

2. **Responsible and conscientious:** ISTJs are likely to be responsible and conscientious in their approach to tasks and obligations, which can make them solid housemates if you value accountability and hard work. Many of them willingly tackle household chores and responsibilities, and they're often willing to take on extra tasks to ensure that everything is taken care of.

3. **Structured and organized:** The structured and organized ISTJ loves order and efficiency. If you need someone to create routines and systems to keep the household running smoothly, turn to an ISTJ. They might show you their organizing and decluttering skills!

4. **Practical and realistic:** ISTJs tend to be practical and realistic in their decision making, appreciating pragmatism and logic. These roommates can help you find practical solutions to problems and conflicts, and they might be able to provide a grounded perspective on difficult situations.

5. **Respectful and considerate:** ISTJs tend to honor rules and traditions, follow household rules and boundaries, and are often willing to compromise to ensure that everyone is comfortable and happy.

The Downside

ISTJs are known for being reliable and responsible roommates, but you might find some of their habits irritating. These traits could include inflexibility, rigidity, perfectionism, discomfort with emotions, and a need for control.

ISTJs can be very set in their ways and may have a hard time adjusting to change. They may resist new ideas or methods of doing things, which can be frustrating for roommates. These housemates can sometimes be too rigid in their thinking and may have a hard time seeing things from different perspectives. You may find an ISTJ roommate being judgmental of others who don't share their values or beliefs, which could be challenging for you. Frequently perfectionists, ISTJ housemates generally have high standards for themselves and others, and they may come across as critical of mistakes or imperfections. This could understandably be demotivating or discouraging for you as a housemate.

In additional, this personality type can sometimes struggle with expressing their emotions diplomatically. They might have trouble telling you that something you're doing is making them uncomfortable, so you may be the one who needs to take the lead on gracefully opening channels of communication when you feel the tension rising. Establishing clear expectations and then respecting each other's boundaries can contribute greatly to a harmonious living experience.

ISTP: "The Pragmatic Adventurer"

The Upside

Living with an ISTP can be an exciting and fulfilling experience, as they're known for their independence, practicality, and problem-solving abilities.

Some reasons why living with an ISTP can be beneficial include their ability to be:

1. **Resourceful and practical:** ISTPs will make ideal housemates if you value efficiency and productivity. Skilled at finding ways to save time and money, they may offer creative solutions to household problems or tasks.

2. **Independent and self-sufficient:** ISTPs can be a perfect match if value privacy and autonomy. They're often quite comfortable with spending time alone, and they're frequently willing to take care of their own needs and responsibilities without relying on others.

3. **Hands-on and skilled:** This type of roommate is often very capable with their hands, which can make them wonderful to work with on DIY projects or home repairs. They may be able to fix things around the house or create new items with ease, and they're oftentimes willing to share their skills with others.

4. **Calm and levelheaded:** ISTPs tend to stay unruffled in their approach to problems or conflicts, which can make them easy to work through issues with. They may be able to provide a rational and logical perspective on difficult situations, helping your household to find a compromise or solution that works for everyone.

5. **Adventurous and spontaneous:** Many ISTPs are adventurous and spontaneous, which you'll appreciate if you relish excitement and new experiences. They might be open to trying new things or

exploring new places as well as encouraging others to step out of their comfort zones.

The Downside

ISTPs are known for being analytical, logical, and action-oriented. However, some potentially irritating habits of an ISTP roommate may include impulsiveness, disorganization, insensitivity, and a lack of communication.

As introverts, ISTPs may have a hard time expressing their thoughts and feelings to others, which can come across as seeming distant, uninterested, or insensitive. However, those impressions may not be accurate, so it's important to try to keep open communication. Some ISTPs can be blunt and direct in their communication and may not always consider how their words or actions affect others.

As perceivers, ISTPs can be spontaneous and enjoy living in the moment. However, this can sometimes lead to impulsive decision making or actions that can be frustrating if you're a planner. While ISTP roommates can be laidback, they may not prioritize organization or cleanliness, perhaps leaving messes or forgetting to complete household chores.

ISTPs can be thrill-seekers and they often enjoy taking risks. However, be aware that this trait can sometimes lead to reckless behavior or dangerous activities that can be concerning for roommates who value safety and security.

ESFJ: "The Loyal Helping Hand"

The Upside

Living with an ESFJ can be a warm and supportive experience, as they're known for their outgoing, friendly, and nurturing personalities. Some of the benefits of living with an ESFJ include their tendency to be:

1. **Supportive and nurturing:** Your ESFJ roommate is likely to be highly supportive and nurturing, providing you with emotional support and encouragement. They're often great at listening, offering advice, and lending a helping hand when you need it.

2. **Sociable and outgoing:** ESFJs are people persons who value social connections and community. Skilled at bringing people together, they may also be great at hosting gatherings and events.

3. **Conscientious and responsible:** ESFJs usually take tasks and obligations seriously, making them accountable and reliable housemates. They'll generally do their share of household chores and responsibilities, and they may also be willing to take on extra tasks to ensure that everything is taken care of.

4. **Attentive and thoughtful:** ESFJs are usually considerate of others' needs and feelings, and they tend to be full of empathy and understanding. They often notice when others need support or help, so they're likely willing to adjust their behavior to ensure that everyone is comfortable and happy.

5. **Traditional and loyal:** ESFJs tend to be stable and consistent as roommates. They usually adhere to household routines and traditions, and their loyalty means that they'll likely stick with you through thick and thin.

The Downside

ESFJs are known for being warm and friendly individuals who value harmony and cooperation. However, some of their negative attributes might include trouble maintaining interpersonal boundaries, an excessive need for approval, a resistance to change, and an inability to say no.

ESFJs can be very caring and concerned about the well-being of their loved ones. That said, they may sometimes come across as intrusive or overbearing, especially if they try to get involved in every aspect of their roommates' lives. ESFJs value social connections and can enjoy discussing the lives of others, but this can sometimes lead to gossip or spreading rumors.

As people-pleasers, they often have a strong desire for approval and validation from others. This can sometimes lead to behavior that may come across as insincere or overly accommodating. They may have a hard time saying no to others, even if it means sacrificing their own needs or wants. This can sometimes lead to over-commitment or taking on more than they can handle, which can be hard for roommates who value boundaries and balance.

Because ESFJs value tradition and stability, they sometimes have a tough time adapting to change, such as resisting new ideas or changes to the household routine.

ESFP: "The Sociable Networker"

The Upside

ESFPs make terrific roommates for several reasons. Some of the benefits of living with an ESFP can be that they're:

1. **Fun and adventurous:** If you value excitement and spontaneity, an ESFP roommate can be an excellent living partner. They're often great at coming up with creative ideas for things to do and are usually willing to try new experiences with their housemates.

2. **Outgoing and sociable:** The friendly ESFP makes a great housemate if you seek social connections and community. Usually quite skilled at making friends and networking, they're known for bringing people together.

3. **Flexible and adaptable:** ESFPs demonstrate versatility and resilience in their approach to life, so as roommates they may be adept at adjusting to changing circumstances and situations—and willing to help you do the same.

4. **Empathetic and supportive:** Often skilled at listening and offering advice, ESFPs are frequently willing to lend a helping hand whenever you need it. They also tend to be quite free with providing emotional support and encouragement.

5. **Creative and expressive:** Your ESFP roommate may be full of artistic expression and creativity, which can come in handy decorating the house, coming up with unique solutions to problems, and bringing their own unique flair to your shared living space.

The Downside

While living with an ESFP can be a fun and exciting experience thanks to their love of adventure, sociability, flexibility, empathy, and creativity, you might also encounter some impulsiveness, messiness, flakiness, loudness, and attention-seeking behavior.

As perceivers, ESFPs can be impulsive and may make decisions without thinking them through. Similarly, they can become so focused on having fun and enjoying the moment that they may neglect their household responsibilities, such as cleaning up after themselves. Some ESFPs can be easily distracted and may struggle with following through on commitments, prompting housemates to think that they're irresponsible.

Because ESFPs tend to be outgoing and extraverted, they may seem loud and boisterous at times, especially if you're an introvert. This can be overwhelming for roommates who prefer a quieter environment. Likewise, ESFPs enjoy being the center of attention and may engage in attention-seeking behavior, such as constantly talking or performing for others, which can be tiring for their roommates.

ISFJ: "The Committed Caretaker"

The Upside

ISFJ housemates bring many positive qualities to a living situation, and some of the best traits of an ISFJ are that they're:

1. **Responsible and reliable:** ISFJs are known to be diligent about their obligations and commitments, which can make them great housemates who are dependable and trustworthy.

2. **Caring and considerate:** They tend to be highly aware of others' needs and feelings. They often go out of their way to make their housemates feel comfortable and supported and may be willing to lend a listening ear or a helping hand when you need it.

3. **Detail-oriented and organized:** ISFJs usually possess a strong attention to detail and organizational skills. They may excel at keeping the living space clean and tidy, often playing an important role in maintaining a well-structured and efficient household.

4. **Patient and calm:** Your ISFJ roommate is likely to have a patient and calm demeanor, which can be helpful in resolving tense situations or conflicts that may arise among housemates. They may be skilled at finding peaceful solutions to problems and promoting harmony within the household.

5. **Loyal and committed:** ISFJs are often known for their strong sense of loyalty and commitment to

their relationships. They might build lasting bonds with their housemates and may be willing to go above and beyond to support and protect those they care about.

The Downside

Living with an ISFJ can be a comfortable and supportive experience, thanks to their sense of responsibility, caring nature, attention to detail, patience, and loyalty. However, some potentially irritating habits of an ISFJ roommate could include being overly accommodating due to their desire to please others and make them comfortable—or, on the other extreme, being inflexible or passive-aggressive.

Your ISFJ roommate may have a tendency to stick to routines and have difficulty adapting to change, which can be challenging if you want to try new things or have different preferences. This personality type may avoid confrontation and instead express their frustrations in subtle or indirect ways, which can lead to misunderstandings and a lack of communication between roommates.

ISFJs can spend a lot of time overthinking their actions and decisions, which sometimes makes them hesitant to take risks or try new things. This can be frustrating if you want to be more spontaneous or adventurous. Also, if you're a perceiver (P), an ISFJ with a strong judging (J) side may have a compelling desire for order and cleanliness, which can lead to them being overly critical or nitpicky about the condition of your shared living space.

ISFP: "The Empathetic Artist"

The Upside

ISFP roommates can bring a great number of positive qualities to your living situation. Some of the best aspects of living with an ISFP is that they're likely to be:

1. **Artistic and creative:** ISFPs often have a unique and imaginative perspective on the world. They may bring a sense of beauty and aesthetic to your living space to create a cozy and comfortable atmosphere.

2. **Easygoing and adaptable:** They're likely willing to compromise and adjust to their housemates' needs and preferences. Being flexible and open to trying new things, they can help create a fun, adventurous environment.

3. **Compassionate and empathetic:** ISFPs tend to have a deep understanding of other people's emotions and perspectives. They're frequently great listeners and supportive friends who are willing to offer a shoulder to cry on or a helping hand when you need it.

4. **Independent and self-sufficient:** An ISFP housemate will likely want to take care of their own needs rather than requiring constant attention or support from their housemates, which can create a low-maintenance living situation.

5. **Peaceful and calming:** They tend to have a peaceful and calming presence that can help create a harmonious living space. They may be skilled at

handling tense situations and promoting a sense of calm and relaxation in the household.

The Downside

An ISFP housemate can be a creative, easygoing, and supportive partner, thanks to their artistic nature, adaptable personality, compassionate spirit, and peaceful demeanor. However, depending upon your own personality, some potentially irritating habits of an ISFP roommate could include what you perceive to be excessive sensitivity, passivity, disorganization, and independence.

ISFPs are often highly attuned to their emotions, which can make them easily upset or offended. This can be frustrating if you feel like you have to tiptoe around them or constantly watch what you say. Also, ISFPs may avoid conflict or confrontation, which can lead to passivity in their interactions. This can be frustrating if you want them to speak up and assert themselves.

As perceivers (Ps), ISFPs sometimes struggle with setting goals and planning, which can lead to last-minute changes or disruptions to their roommate's plans. They may prioritize their creative pursuits over household chores, which can lead to a messy or disorganized living space.

As introverts, ISFPs might prioritize their alone time and creative pursuits over spending time with you or other members of the household, which can lead to feelings of isolation or neglect among their roommates. If you're a strong extravert, you might perceive your ISFP roommate as withdrawn or even rude for not spending enough time with you, but it's important not to take it personally and to realize that you each have different expectations and needs for personal space.

This chapter covered a lot of ground, but the most significant actions to take in terms of getting along well with anyone you share a living space with are using communication strategies that affirm their needs while also clearly articulating your own, then trying to find a solution that satisfies both of you. Personality types can be as different as they can be complimentary, but with an open mind and an ability to empathize and anticipate one another's wants and desires, you and your housemates can be a match made in domestic heaven!

Faith Fuson

And What About Me? How Can I Be the Best Roommate Given My Personality Type?

WHILE THE PREVIOUS chapter was primarily focused on your housemate's personality, I left hints along the way to indicate that the key to understanding roommate relationships is in looking at the dynamics of the interplay of the two (or more) personalities in the household. Both harmony and conflict arise from the interaction of your personality and its preferences with those of the person you're living with.

In this chapter, let's hold up a mirror and look at yourself, answering the following questions: How you can draw upon your personality type, and what do you need to work on to be the best roommate or housemate you can be?

As in the previous chapter, let's emphasize that very few people live together in harmony without needing to put forth an effort (on both sides) to be considerate of each other's needs and, most importantly, to communicate clearly about those needs in a way that helps the other person become more aware. You'll never find the perfect roommate "right out of the box"—it's a bit more complicated than buying a pair of shoes! Instead, the most important trait in a potential living partner is the willingness to work at being a good roommate or housemate—to communicate clearly and to negotiate to find common ground.

ENTJ: "The House Manager"

As an ENTJ, you can do several things to draw upon your personality type to become a considerate roommate. Below are a few tips to keep in mind about how people with your personality type can be terrific housemates:

1. **Be organized:** You're probably orderly and structured, so use this trait to keep your living space clean and tidy. Make sure your belongings are put away and don't take up too much space in common areas.

2. **Be respectful:** Self-confident ENTJs can come across as assertive or intimidating, so seek to be respectful of your housemates' boundaries and feelings. Even though you may feel sure that your way is the best way, listen to their concerns and opinions—and be willing to compromise when necessary. Remember to remain open to learning from your housemates and finding ways to work together effectively.

3. **Be responsible:** ENTJs tend to be reliable and dependable, so take on your fair share of household chores and contribute to the household in meaningful ways. Be punctual and follow through on your commitments.

4. **Communicate openly:** You may be direct and straightforward in your communication style, so use this trait to communicate openly and honestly with your housemates. Always be diplomatic (which is sometimes a challenge for "take charge" ENTJs). Address any concerns or issues in a timely manner and be willing to have difficult conversations when necessary. Be sure not to communicate in a blaming or condescending way, but instead work to listen and truly hear your roommate and their needs and concerns.

5. **Be flexible:** As an ENTJ, you may be focused on achieving your goals, so strive to be flexible and adaptable when it comes to household routines and schedules. Be willing to compromise and adjust to accommodate your housemates' needs.

However, your assertiveness may come across as bossy or controlling, which can strain relationships with your roommates. Additionally, your focus on achieving goals may make it harder for you to prioritize and compromise when it comes to shared living spaces and responsibilities.

To be a great roommate as an ENTJ, you can work on developing your empathy and communication skills. Practice actively listening to your roommates' concerns and opinions, and always stay open to their perspectives when making decisions. Learn to communicate assertively but respectfully, and avoid dominating conversations or steamrolling over others' ideas.

You can also strive to be flexible and adaptable, recognizing that compromise and cooperation are important for maintaining positive relationships with your roommates. Avoid being rigid or overly focused on your own priorities at the expense of others, and be willing to make adjustments to your plans and routines when necessary.

ENTP: "The Easygoing Problem Solver"

As an ENTP, you'll be able to draw upon your natural curiosity, creativity, and adaptability to be an engaging and effective roommate. Your love of exploring new ideas and experiences can bring a sense of fun and excitement to your household.

Some areas that you may need to work on in order to be a good ENTP roommate include:

1. **Responsibility:** You can be easily distracted by new ideas and may struggle to follow through on commitments or household chores. To be a fantastic roommate, be sure to work on being responsible and reliable.

2. **Sensitivity:** At times, you're likely to be blunt and direct, which housemates might perceive as insensitivity. Be sure to prioritize being considerate of your roommates' feelings by communicating tactfully. Be aware that your love of debate and devil's advocacy may come across as argumentative or confrontational, which can be off-putting to some.

3. **Punctuality:** You tend to be flexible with time and may not prioritize punctuality, but being late or unreliable can be frustrating for the people who

depend on you. To be an excellent roommate, be sure to work on being punctual and respecting the other person's time.

4. **Cleanliness:** As an ENTP, you might not prioritize cleanliness as much as your roommate does, which can cause tension. Always work on being more mindful of keeping shared spaces clean and contributing to household chores, even if it doesn't feel like a priority to you. Your likely tendency to procrastinate or avoid routine tasks may create tension if your roommates feel like they're picking up the slack.

5. **Compromise:** You may frequently prioritize your own needs and interests over what's best for the household, which can understandably lead to conflicts. To be a good roommate, work on your willingness to compromise in order to find solutions that work for everyone.

To be an awesome roommate as an ENTP, you can work on developing your communication and responsibility skills. Practice expressing your opinions and ideas in a way that's respectful and collaborative rather than dismissive or challenging. Learn to recognize when your communication style may be creating unnecessary conflict, and try to focus on finding common ground instead.

You can also strive to be reliable and proactive in your household responsibilities. Recognize that your roommates may have different priorities or preferences, so be willing to work together to find solutions that work for everyone.

INTJ: "The Respectful Organizer"

As an INTJ, you possess many desirable attributes that'll make you an appealing roommate. You're respectful, well organized, and you can be a good communicator. Here are a few tips to help you draw upon your best characteristics when you're living with someone else:

1. **Be organized:** You're likely to be organized and structured, so use this trait to keep your living space clean and tidy. Make sure to put your belongings away, and don't take up too much space in common areas.

2. **Be respectful:** Sometimes INTJs can come across as aloof or cold, so try to be respectful of your roommates' feelings and boundaries. Listen to their concerns and opinions and be willing to compromise when necessary.

3. **Be responsible:** As an INTJ, you tend to be reliable and responsible, so take on your fair share of household chores. Contribute to the household in meaningful ways by being punctual and following through on your commitments.

4. **Communicate openly:** With your personality type, you tend to be direct and to-the-point, so use this trait to communicate openly and honestly with your roommates—but also be diplomatic and listen closely to the other person's perspectives. Address any concerns or issues in a timely manner and be willing to have difficult conversations when necessary.

5. **Be independent:** INTJs tend to be independent and self-sufficient, so use this skill to take care of your own needs and space. You won't rely too heavily on your roommates for emotional support or companionship. This can have its positive and negative sides, depending upon how extraverted (E) or feeling-centered (F) your roommates are. They may want more of a relationship from you.

Keep in mind, however, that some of your strongest traits also have a flipside that can make you hard to live with for someone who has an opposite personality type. For example, as an INTJ, you tend to be logical and rational, but you may come across as insensitive to your roommate's feelings. To be a better roommate, you might need to work on being more considerate and empathetic.

Another area to be aware of is staying flexible. As an INTJ, you tend to be rigid in your thinking and may struggle with adapting to changes or compromising with your housemates, so remember to work on being more flexible and open-minded. You might also tend to be impatient with other people, especially when you live with them, so it may take some extra effort to be patient and adapt to their personalities and styles.

Also, be self-reflective about your social skills. As introverts, some INTJs may struggle with social interactions, which can make it difficult to connect with your roommate. To improve your relationship, you can work on developing relationships with your housemates.

INTP: "The Adaptable Peacemaker"

As an INTP, your personality type provides you with lots of significant skills to be an enjoyable and responsible roommate. The following list is a reminder of how you can use your natural preferences and abilities to get along with the ones you live with:

1. **Be adaptable:** You tend to be flexible and open-minded, so use this trait to adapt to your roommates' habits and preferences. Be willing to compromise and find solutions that work for everyone.

2. **Be respectful:** You tend to value privacy and independence, but don't forget to be respectful of your roommates' boundaries and needs. Listen to their concerns and opinions and be willing to make changes when necessary.

3. **Be reliable:** Since you might sometimes be forgetful or absentminded, be sure to make an effort to be reliable and follow through on your commitments. Stay responsible for your share of household chores and contribute to the household in meaningful ways.

4. **Communicate clearly:** As a logical and analytical person, you can use this skill to communicate clearly and effectively with your roommates. Be open and honest about any concerns or issues and be willing to have difficult conversations when necessary.

5. **Be independent but cooperative:** As an INTP, you value independence and autonomy, so you'll have no trouble maintaining your boundaries

and respecting your roommates' space and privacy as well. However, try your best to be sociable and strive to spend some time together in the shared spaces.

Because of your configuration of INTP personality traits, you may need to make a special effort to work on certain skills to be a good roommate. These include cleanliness, sensitivity, punctuality, and social skills.

INTPs tend to prioritize their own interests over household chores, which can cause tension with more cleanliness-oriented roommates. To be a great roommate, you can focus on being mindful of keeping shared spaces clean and contributing to household chores.

Personality-wise, as a INTP you might come across as blunt or insensitive in your interactions, so many INTPs need to work on being more considerate of their roommates' feelings and how their words can affect others. As an introvert, you may struggle with social interactions, which can make it difficult to connect with roommates. You can become a better roommate by developing your social skills and putting an effort into building a relationship.

INTPs can be flexible with time and may not prioritize punctuality. In a living situation, being late or unreliable (or procrastinating) can be frustrating for roommates, so you may need to work harder at being punctual and respecting your housemates' time.

ENFJ: "The Compassionate Social Manager"

As an ENFJ housemate, you can draw upon your natural warmth, empathy, and social skills to create a welcoming and harmonious living space. You may enjoy fostering close relationships with your roommates, and you can be a supportive and caring presence in the household.

Some specific ways you can draw upon your personality type as an ENFJ to be a good roommate are to exercise your strengths:

1. **Foster close relationships** with your roommates by showing warmth, empathy, and a genuine interest in their lives.
2. **Create a welcoming and harmonious living space** by being attentive to your roommates' needs and concerns.
3. **Offer emotional support and encouragement** when your roommates are going through difficult times.
4. **Be a positive and uplifting presence** in the household, bringing a sense of joy and optimism to your interactions with others.

However, your desire for harmony and people-pleasing may make it difficult for you to assert your own needs or boundaries, which can lead to resentment or conflict. Additionally, your focus on relationships and emotions can hinder your ability to address practical or logistical issues or conflicts that arise in your living space.

Some areas you can work on that will achieve great gains in your roommate relationship as an ENFJ include developing your assertiveness and practical skills. Practice asserting your own needs and boundaries in a clear and respectful way, even if it may cause temporary discomfort. Develop practical skills like scheduling, cleaning, and organizing, and be willing to take charge of these tasks as necessary.

You can also use your skills to create a supportive and positive living environment for your roommates. Try to balance your focus on relationships with a practical approach to problem solving. Be mindful of not sacrificing your own well-being for the sake of others, as this can lead to resentment or burnout. Avoid becoming overly involved in your roommates' personal lives or conflicts, which can create drama and tension in your living space. That said, make sure to be available to offer a listening ear or a shoulder to lean on when necessary. Practice active listening and emotional support, and you'll make valuable inroads into being an awesome roommate.

ENFP: "The Enthusiastic Motivator"

As an ENFP, your natural creativity, empathy, and communication skills can help to create a fun and positive living environment for yourself and your roommates. You may enjoy exploring new ideas and experiences, and your enthusiasm can inspire and energize those around you.

To be a good roommate as an ENFP, you can work on balancing your strengths with practical responsibilities and clear communication. Below are some specific ways to draw upon your strengths:

1. **Use your creativity** to make your living space unique and inspiring, incorporating personal touches and fun decorations.

2. **Show empathy and understanding** toward your roommates, being attuned to their emotional needs and supporting them when they need it.

3. **Use your natural communication skills** to foster open and honest dialogue with your roommates, encouraging everyone to share their thoughts and feelings.

4. **Bring a sense of joy and spontaneity** to your interactions with others, creating a positive and uplifting atmosphere in your home.

However, your tendency to be distracted by new ideas and opportunities can make it easy to neglect practical responsibilities like housecleaning or doing laundry. Additionally, your desire for harmony and avoiding conflict can make it hard for you to assert your own needs or address issues that arise in the household. Be willing to assert those needs or discuss conflicts that arise in a clear, respectful way.

One area to work on is being more proactive with practical responsibilities like cleaning, paying bills, and maintaining household items. Set reminders for yourself or create schedules if necessary. Practice being more organized and structured in your approach to tasks and responsibilities, balancing your creativity with practical considerations.

Another area that may need attention is recognizing the importance of boundaries. Be mindful of not overwhelming your roommates with too much activity or excitement, recognizing that they may have different needs for downtime and relaxation.

INFJ: "The Empathetic Mediator"

As an INFJ, you can draw upon your natural empathy, intuition, and focus on harmony to create a peaceful and supportive living environment for yourself and your roommates. You may enjoy deep conversations and personal connections, and you can use your insights to understand and connect with those around you.

To be a great roommate, work on balancing your strengths with practical responsibilities and clear communication. Here are some specific ways to draw upon your strengths:

1. **Be empathetic** toward your roommates. Stay attuned to their emotional needs and offer support to them whenever the need arises.

2. **Use your intuition and insights** to create a welcoming and peaceful living environment, incorporating calming elements like plants, candles, or soft lighting.

3. **Foster deep and meaningful connections** with your roommates by engaging in personal conversations and sharing your experiences and perspectives.

4. **Create a sense of harmony** in your living space by being respectful and considerate of your roommates' needs and preferences.

However, your desire for harmony may make it difficult for you to address conflicts or assert your own needs, which can make the situation worse. Additionally, your tendency to be introspective and private may make it challenging to engage in social activities or communicate openly with your roommates. Practice being more assertive when necessary, recognizing that conflicts or misunderstandings may arise and addressing them in a respectful and clear way.

Be mindful of not isolating yourself too much, recognizing the importance of engaging with your roommates and contributing to a positive and social atmosphere in your living space. Be willing to engage in social activities or outings with your roommates, recognizing the value of building relationships outside of the home.

Practice being more proactive with essential responsibilities like cleaning, paying bills, and maintaining household items. Sett reminders for yourself or develop schedules if necessary. You may want to procrastinate or avoid these activities since you have more desirable things to do, but realize that when you live with others, staying on top of tasks becomes an important priority.

INFP: "The Considerate Collaborator"

As an INFP, you can draw upon your natural creativity and empathy, as well as focus on your personal values to create a warm and welcoming living environment for yourself and your roommates. You can use your sensitivity to connect with and understand those around you. To be a super roommate as an INFP, you can work on balancing your strengths with practical responsibilities and clear communication. Below are some specific ways to do this:

1. **Use your creativity** to make your living space unique and inspiring, incorporating personal touches and elements that reflect your personal values.

2. **Show empathy and understanding** toward your roommates, being attuned to their emotional needs and supporting them when they need it.

3. **Foster deep and meaningful connections** with your roommates by engaging in personal conversations and sharing your insights and perspectives.

4. **Create a welcoming and comfortable living environment** by paying attention to small details like lighting, colors, and textures.

However, your ENFP tendency toward introspection and privacy may make it challenging to engage in social activities or communicate openly with your roommates. Additionally, your focus on personal values may make it difficult for you to compromise or adapt to others' needs and preferences.

Be mindful of not isolating yourself too much, recognizing the importance of engaging with your roommates and contributing to a positive and social atmosphere in your living space. Even though you're an introvert and prefer spending a lot of time alone, be willing to engage in social activities or outings with your roommate or housemates, recognizing the value of building these distinctive relationships. You may need to explain your personality type to more extraverted housemates if they think your spending too much time alone is a sign of lack of friendliness or interest in them.

Do your share, and do it on time. Become more proactive with practical responsibilities like cleaning, paying bills, and maintaining the household. Even if you find these tasks distasteful or boring, do whatever you can to stay on top of them by setting reminders or schedules if necessary. Try to overcome your tendency to procrastinate. Practice being more flexible and adaptable to others' needs and preferences, recognizing the importance of compromise and collaboration in a shared living space.

ESTJ: "The Structured Goal-Setter"

As an ESTJ, you can draw upon your natural organization, leadership, and practicality to create an efficient and effective living environment for yourself and your roommates. You may enjoy establishing routines and systems to keep things running smoothly, and you can use your straightforward and direct communication style to resolve conflicts.

To be an excellent roommate as an ESTJ, you can work on balancing your strengths with consideration for your roommates' needs and preferences. Below are some specific ways to do this:

5. **Establish clear expectations and systems** for household tasks and responsibilities, using your practicality and organization to create an efficient living environment.

6. **Use your direct and assertive communication style** to address conflicts or issues as they arise, and work toward finding practical and effective solutions.

7. **Show loyalty and dependability** toward your roommates, following through on commitments and being a reliable member of the household.

8. **Use your leadership skills** to motivate and inspire your roommates to contribute to the household and work toward common goals.

However, your focus on efficiency and productivity may make it difficult to relax and enjoy downtime with your roommates. Additionally, your direct communication style may come across as harsh or critical to others, so you might want to work on being more sensitive to their emotional needs and preferences.

Practice being more sensitive to your roommates' emotional needs and preferences, recognizing that not everyone responds well to direct or critical communication. Make an extra effort to be diplomatic in your communication style, and prioritize developing your listening skills so that you don't come across as too assertive or demanding. Be willing to compromise and adapt to others' needs and preferences, recognizing that a shared living space requires collaboration and consideration.

Be more open to new experiences and perspectives, recognizing that your rigid adherence to routine and tradition may limit your ability to connect with and understand others. Be mindful of not overworking or neglecting your own self-care and personal relationships, recognizing the importance of downtime and relaxation.

ESTP: "The Fun-Loving Companion"

As an ESTP, you can draw upon your natural energy, spontaneity, and adaptability to create an exciting and engaging living environment for yourself and your roommates. You may enjoy trying new things, exploring the world around you, and approaching life with a sense of fun and excitement.

However, spontaneity and lack of planning may make it difficult for your roommates to know what to expect or keep up with your pace. Additionally, your preference for taking risks and living in the moment may conflict with others' desire for stability and predictability.

To be a great roommate as an ESTP, you can work on balancing your strengths with consideration for your roommates' needs and preferences. The following are some specific ways to do this:

1. **Use your energy and enthusiasm** to create a fun and engaging living environment, encouraging your roommates to join you in new experiences and adventures.

2. **Be adaptable and flexible**—roll with the punches and adjust to changes as they arise.
3. **Use your practicality and resourcefulness** to handle household tasks and responsibilities efficiently and effectively.
4. **Use your straightforward and direct communication style** to address conflicts or issues as they arise, working toward finding practical and effective solutions.

Some areas where you may need to make a special effort—since these behaviors may not come naturally to you—can include being more mindful of the schedules and preferences of those you live with. It's important to recognize that your preference for spontaneity and lack of planning may be disruptive or overwhelming to others.

Practice being more patient and considerate, recognizing that not everyone shares your desire for risk-taking or living in the moment, which can actually cause others anxiety. Be more attentive to the impact of your actions on others, understanding that your behavior may affect the comfort and well-being of your roommates. Similarly, stay willing to compromise and adapt to others' needs and preferences, recognizing that a shared living space requires collaboration and consideration.

ISTJ: "The Reliable Organizer"

If your test results reveal you to be an ISTJ personality type, you're likely to approach your living space with a practical and organized mindset, ensuring that everything is in its proper place and running smoothly. These are highly valued traits in a housemate. You're generally straightforward and direct in your communication, expressing your needs and expectations clearly and listening actively to others, which can help you avoid misunderstandings and conflicts with roommates.

To be the best roommate you can be, draw upon your strengths while also being mindful of potential challenges that may arise. Here are some specific ways to accentuate your best characteristics:

1. **Use your reliability and responsibility** to ensure that you take care of household tasks and responsibilities efficiently and effectively.

2. **Draw upon your attention to detail** to keep the shared living space clean and organized, ensuring that everything is in its proper place.

3. **Use your practical and logical approach** to handle conflicts or issues that may arise, working toward finding effective solutions that make everyone happy.

4. **Be respectful of your roommates' space and privacy**, recognizing the importance of boundaries and personal preferences.

However, there are some areas that ISTJs might want to work on, and they include being more:

- flexible and adaptable, recognizing that not everyone has the same approach to organization and structure as you do

- open-minded and accepting of different viewpoints and ways of doing things; there may be more than one "right" way
- communicative and expressive, understanding that your reserved nature may sometimes come across as cold or distant
- willing to compromise and collaborate with your roommates, appreciating that a shared living space requires give-and-take and consideration for others

ISTP: "The Pragmatic Adventurer"

As an ISTP, you bring many strengths that can make you a great roommate, including your independence, adaptability, and practical problem-solving skills. You're likely to approach your living space with a logical and hands-on mindset, ensuring that everything is working smoothly and efficiently. Your roommate or housemates will definitely appreciate all that you have to offer.

To be an ideal ISTP roommate, lean upon your strengths but also be aware of potential issues that frequently arise for roommates of your personality type when living with others. To leverage your strengths to their best advantage:

1. **Use your independence and self-sufficiency** to take care of your own needs and responsibilities, without relying too heavily on your roommates. However, be aware of the fine line between independence and interdependence as you remember that living with another person requires the latter.

This means not pulling into your own shell too much, as it will likely come at the expense of having a pleasant relationship with your roommate.

2. **Draw upon your practical problem-solving skills** to fix any issues that arise in your living space, such as a broken appliance or a leaky faucet. The S and P combination in your personality type makes you a terrific troubleshooter, a role that's highly valuable in life and around the house.

3. **Use your adaptability** to handle changes or unexpected situations that may arise, such as a roommate moving out unexpectedly. One advantage of your type is that you can deal well with change, which is much more challenging for other personalities (especially for Js).

4. **Be respectful of your roommates' boundaries and personal preferences**, recognizing the importance of privacy and personal space.

Some other things, however, may require a bit of extra effort on your part. You might want to focus on being more:

- communicative and expressive, aware that your reserved nature may sometimes come across as distant or uninterested in your roommates
- considerate of your roommates' needs and preferences, recognizing that a shared living space requires give-and-take and compromise.
- attentive to the emotional atmosphere of your living space, understanding that your tendency

to focus on practical matters may sometimes overlook the emotional needs of your roommates
- proactive in addressing potential conflicts or issues with your roommates, realizing that your tendency to avoid confrontation may sometimes create tension or resentment.

ESFJ: "The Loyal Helping Hand"

As an ESFJ, you possess many positive and endearing traits—such as being friendly, nurturing, and empathetic—that will make you a desirable roommate. You're likely attuned to the needs and emotions of those around you, which can make you a supportive and caring presence. Below are some specific ways you can use your existing character traits to be a great roommate:

1. **Communicate openly and honestly:** ESFJs are typically good communicators and value harmony in their relationships. Ideally, you'll communicate openly and honestly about your needs and expectations and actively listen to your roommate's concerns. You may find it helpful to establish clear boundaries and agreements about shared spaces, cleaning schedules, and other household tasks.

2. **Show empathy and understanding:** ESFJs are known for their ability to empathize with others and to be supportive in times of need. If your roommate is going through a tough time, you'll be there to listen and offer emotional support. You may also want to be mindful of your own behavior and how it might impact your roommate's well-being.

3. **Be organized and responsible:** You're organized and responsible, which can be helpful in maintaining a tidy and functional living space. You may find it helpful to establish a cleaning schedule and to make sure that household chores are divided fairly between you and your roommate.

However, be aware of your tendency to put others' needs before your own: ESFJs often prioritize other people over themselves, which can lead to burnout or resentment on your part. It's important to take care of your own needs and to communicate clearly when you need support or help.

You also may want to practice assertiveness. ESFJs sometimes tend to avoid conflict in order to maintain harmony in their relationships. However, doing so can lead to a buildup of resentment or unaddressed issues. Practice asserting your needs and boundaries in a clear and respectful way.

Finally, be sure to allow for flexibility and compromise. You may have strong opinions about how things should be done, but it's important to be open to your living partner's ideas in order to maintain a harmonious living environment. Be willing to listen to your roommate's perspective and to negotiate solutions that work for both of you.

ESFP: "The Sociable Networker"

Your natural ESFP traits as an outgoing, fun-loving, and adaptable roommate will take you a long way in building an ideal living situation. You likely have a contagious energy and a talent for creating a positive atmosphere, which can make you a great person to live with. The following are some specific ways you can use your personality type to be an excellent roommate:

1. **Be sociable and welcoming:** ESFPs are typically sociable and enjoy being around other people. To be a great roommate, you can use your outgoing personality to create a welcoming atmosphere in your home. You may want to organize social events or gatherings or simply be open to spending time with your housemates.

2. **Be adaptable and flexible:** Being able to adapt to new situations is a terrific skill when moving in with a new person or household, since you'll need to be willing to compromise and adjust to your roommate's needs and preferences.

3. **Bring positivity and fun to the home:** If you're like most ESFPs, you're fun-loving and energetic, and many people find you a joy to be around! You can use this trait to bring positivity and fun to your household, whether it's by planning fun activities or simply having a positive attitude.

Despite being a force of positive energy, you'll need to stay aware of your tendency to prioritize enjoyment over responsibilities. ESFPs may sometimes place having fun as a priority over taking care of business, which can cause conflict if others see you as irresponsible. It's important to find a balance between enjoying yourself and taking care of your responsibilities.

Also, practice communication and conflict resolution. ESFPs tend to avoid conflict or difficult conversations in order to always maintain an upbeat atmosphere. However, issues that go unaddressed can escalate over time. Practice communicating openly and respectfully, and be willing to address conflicts in a timely and productive manner.

As an ESFP, be mindful of boundaries and personal space. Since you tend to be outgoing and energetic, you might sometimes cross over boundaries into others' personal space. Be mindful of your roommate's preferences, especially in terms of respecting their need for personal space and quiet time.

ISFJ: "The Committed Caretaker"

As an ISFJ roommate, you'll be bringing to the table your natural traits of being responsible, reliable, and caring. You'll probably be sensitive to your roommate's needs and emotions, and you may prioritize creating a comfortable and harmonious living environment. Some specific ways you can use your personality type to be a great roommate include:

1. **Being reliable and responsible:** ISFJs are usually dependable and responsible, which are valuable traits in a roommate. You may want to establish clear agreements about household chores, bills, and other responsibilities, always making sure to follow through on your commitments.

2. **Showing consideration and thoughtfulness:** Because of your caring and thoughtful nature, you'll be sure to show consideration for your

roommate's needs and preferences, whether it's by cleaning up after yourself, respecting their personal space, or simply being there for them when they need support.

3. **Creating a harmonious living environment:** ISFJs tend to value harmony and stability in their relationships and environments. You can use this skill to create a comfortable and peaceful living space for you and your roommate, whether it's by decorating the space in a soothing way, organizing shared spaces in a thoughtful manner, or simply being a calming presence in the home.

However, you might want to work on practicing assertiveness and boundary-setting since you may sometimes struggle with asserting your own needs and setting boundaries, which can lead you to feel resentment or frustration. Practice communicating your needs and preferences in a clear and respectful way and be willing to establish your boundaries whenever necessary.

Also, be mindful of your tendency to overcommit. As an ISFJ, you may take on too much responsibility or put others' needs before your own, which can lead to burnout. It's important to exercise self-care and to communicate clearly when you need support or help.

Finally, practice flexibility and adaptability. You may tend to stick to routines or established ways of doing things, which can be challenging in a roommate situation where compromise is often necessary. Stay open to new ideas and approaches and be willing to adapt to your roommate's needs and preferences when appropriate.

ISFP: "The Empathetic Artist"

Your personality type as an ISFP means that you're creative, sensitive, and flexible, which are terrific qualities to have as a roommate. You likely have a strong sense of style and may enjoy creating a comfortable and visually appealing living space. The following are some specific ways you can use your personality type to be an excellent roommate:

1. **Use your creativity to enhance your living space:** ISFPs often have a strong sense of aesthetics and creativity. Use this sensibility to create a comfortable and visually appealing living space for you and your roommate—with their input, of course. You may want to decorate the space with art or other visually interesting items, or simply use your creativity to find unique solutions to practical problems.

2. **Be sensitive to your roommate's needs and emotions:** As an ISFP, you tend to be sensitive and empathetic, which can be valuable traits when you live with someone. Pay attention to your roommate's emotional state and be supportive when they need it.

3. **Be adaptable and flexible:** You'll have no trouble being willing to compromise, adjusting to your roommate's needs and preferences, being open to trying new things, and approaching problems in a different way.

That said, be mindful of your tendency to avoid conflict—ISFPs may sometimes avoid uncomfortable conversations and situations because they don't want to disrupt a peaceful atmosphere. This can lead to issues going unaddressed or escalating over time, so work on communicating with your roommate openly and respectfully, and be willing to address any conflicts in a timely and productive manner. You'll find that resolving tension when it first begins is much easier than letting it build.

Practice organization and taking care of essential responsibilities, an area that ISFPs sometimes struggle with. Try to develop systems or routines to stay organized, and make sure to follow through on your commitments.

Lastly, be mindful of your need for personal space. ISFPs tend to value their personal space and independence, which can sometimes cause conflict with a roommate who has different needs and might make you feel crowded. Be clear about your boundaries and preferences, but also be respectful of your roommate's need for connection as well.

Phew! That was another doozy of a chapter, loaded with plenty of pertinent info related to your own personality type and the special dynamic that you bring to the proverbial table. No matter where you fall on the personality type scale, you're bound to be a memorable housemate with your own distinctive personality and unique way of approaching all kinds of situations. And as long as you stay attuned to your roommate's personality type and personal needs and communicate clearly with them, you'll be on track to having a wonderful living experience together.

Faith Fuson

Communication Styles and Skills

"*MY ROOMMATE IS the silent type. She just withdraws whenever she senses that I'm frustrated with her. She avoids me, and then the tension just gets worse.*"

"*I have this one housemate who's a cool person in general, but he's...well, to put it nicely, disorganized. No, it's more than that. He's a slob. And I keep dropping hints, but he doesn't seem to pick up on them. I'm sick of living in his mess. I'm not his mom, and I'm not going to clean up after him.*"

"*My college roommate makes me uncomfortable. She's really needy and clingy. I'm so excited to be in college and making new friends in classes and on my sports team, but my roommate gets jealous when I do things with new friends and acts like I should always be including her or doing things with her.*"

"*I'm a very busy person. I run a tight schedule and need to get a lot done in a short time. The problem is my roommate. She's totally undependable. I mean, I like her as a person, but she never follows up on doing her share of the chores, and I can't even count on her to be punctual when we set an appointment or when it's time to pay the bills. It's like she lives in a different reality than I do!*"

"*I really, really enjoy my housemate as a friend when I need somebody to talk to, but he's not around half the time. Sometimes, he'll just disappear for a few days without telling me, and then I worry that he's hurt or something. When I text him, he doesn't respond. He just assumes I'll take care of his cat while he's gone, but he's never even asked me! Is this normal?"*

It all comes down to communication! When two or more people live together, they each bring expectations of what a roommate should be and how a roommate should act. But if those expectations aren't on the same page (and they're usually not), then tensions are bound to arise.

Are these problems relationship-killers for people sharing a living space? Actually, not at all! Each one of the above issues can easily be solved if the housemates or roommates sit down and clearly explain their needs and expectations to the other person. Learning about personality types (as covered in Chapters 5 to 7) can also be extremely helpful.

If two people are committed to trying to be the best roommates they can be, then all it takes is working on communication skills, avoiding toxic interpersonal behaviors, and the willingness to compromise and negotiate to find a mutually satisfying solution. But you'll never be able to find that solution if you don't talk to each other—in person, and not by leaving notes on the bathroom mirror or sending texts.

What is the goal of skilled, effective communication, and why is it so important in relationships between housemates or roommates?

The goal of communication is to convey your ideas clearly and accurately to others while also actively listening to and understanding their perspectives.

Effective communication contributes to building positive relationships, preventing misunderstandings and conflicts, and promoting mutual understanding and respect.

In relationships between housemates or roommates, effective communication is highly important, because you share a living space and need to make decisions together about aspects of daily life, household responsibilities, finances, and other issues. Poor communication can lead to misunderstandings, disagreements, and conflicts that can negatively impact the living situation and strain—or even end—the relationship.

Effective communication involves being open and honest with each other, actively listening to one another's concerns, and finding mutually acceptable solutions to problems as they arise. It also involves respecting each other's boundaries and preferences, being considerate of each other's needs, and communicating in a way that's respectful and non-judgmental.

In short, effective communication skills are essential for building positive and healthy relationships between roommates.

A Special Kind of Relationship

As roommates, you and the other person(s) are in a distinctive type of relationship which, as mentioned in an earlier chapter, occupies a niche all its own. It's not necessarily a friendship and it's not a work relationship—but it is, in many cases, a transactional, business-type of relationship that you can conceptualize in contractual terms. That's why having a Roommate Agreement can be so significant.

Essentially, it's crucial to take the concept of affection—whether it be liking or loving a person—out of the equation. Of course, many roommates do become BFFs—but that's in addition to their roommate relationship, not an integral part of it. You can have a perfectly successful roommate relationship with someone you don't feel a bond of affection or friendship with as long as you have mutual respect, civility, and pleasant communication.

Norms of Civil Interaction

In the United States, our norms of civil interaction are the generally accepted rules or standards that govern how people should behave when interacting with others in social and public settings. These benchmarks are essential for promoting respectful and harmonious interactions among individuals and groups. Some examples include:

- **Respect for others:** This involves treating others with dignity, kindness, and empathy. It means avoiding behaviors such as insulting, belittling, or disparaging.
- **Listening actively:** Listening is a crucial aspect of civil interaction. It means paying attention to what others are saying, asking questions, and responding thoughtfully.
- **Speaking considerately:** When communicating with others, it's important to use a respectful tone

and avoid using offensive language or making personal attacks.
- **Giving space:** Allowing others personal space and respecting their boundaries is an essential aspect of civil interaction. This means avoiding intrusive behaviors, such as touching others without permission or invading their personal area.
- **Honesty:** Being honest and transparent in our interactions with others is imperative for building trust and maintaining healthy relationships.
- **Accountability:** Taking responsibility for our actions and apologizing when we've caused harm is critical for repairing relationships and promoting reconciliation.

There are many other norms that contribute to creating a respectful and harmonious social environment, and they vary across different cultures and social contexts.

What I want you to take away from this chapter is the fact that these norms—which apply to how we learn to interact with strangers, acquaintances, classmates, neighbors, and people in service professions that we interact with on a daily basis—are the very same norms that undergird a strong roommate relationship.

Violations of Norms for Civil Interaction

In our society, when people violate these norms in a social or public relationship, our reaction is to label them as thoughtless, rude, inconsiderate, disruptive, aggressive, or even abusive, depending upon the degree to which they violate these norms. The latter two are especially egregious: aggressive behavior describes someone who uses forceful or threatening behavior toward others, while abusive behavior refers to someone who exercises harmful or hurtful behavior that might be physical, emotional, or verbal.

Thoughtless ------ Rude ----- Inconsiderate ------ Disruptive ------ Aggressive ------ Abusive

I mention these violation levels because in situations when you're living with another person, slipping into what a roommate might perceive as rude or inconsiderate behavior—or even disruptive behavior—isn't uncommon if you're not conscientiously keeping your need for respectfulness front of mind.

People who concentrate on fulfilling their own needs without considering the effects of their actions or the needs of the other person they live with often slide into these zones. These are danger signals that your relationship needs some work if it's going to succeed. You need to turn things around. And this requires sensitivity and diplomatic communication skills.

Let me pause for a moment and state, without hesitation, that if you find yourself in an abusive relationship with anyone, you should remove yourself from that relationship as quickly as you can. When things get abusive, they're beyond your ability to healthily "fix" things. Seek help and exit the relationship.

However, if you've been self-reflecting as you've read the last few pages, you may recognize your own actions—or the actions of your housemate—as falling into one or more of these violation categories from time to time, or even on a regular basis. The more this happens, the more toxic and unhealthier the relationship becomes.

Acknowledging that a problem exists and seeking to change your own behavior is definitely a promising first step. But remember that it takes work, and it needs to be consistently in the forefront of your thoughts and intentions.

It also takes two to change a relationship. Any changes that you personally make need to be accompanied by open verbal communication to your roommate that acknowledges your newfound awareness. It requires making a mutual commitment to improve the relationship on both of your parts.

Even if one person has remained civil and courteous while their roommate has slipped into inconsiderate or disruptive behavior, they've likely built up some anger or resentment (or even fear) as a response to the way their housemate has treated them. Therefore, it'll take efforts on both sides to "reset" the relationship so that it feels harmonious and so that trust gets established on both sides.

Depending upon the length of time that these violations have been occurring, the partner who has been on the receiving end may decide that they're unwilling to try to make it work. That's a fair response, since being the victim of rudeness and aggression for too long can make one lose respect for the other person and decrease the motivation to try to fix things. In that case, seeking help from a third party or ending the living arrangement is a reasonable solution.

My purpose in writing this book is to help you learn skills and gain understanding that will prevent you from getting to that point of no return. Hopefully, you're reading this book at a point when you can preemptively apply these concepts to your own behaviors and gain communicative competence so that you'll become a positive force in your roommate relationship from early on in the process.

Communicative Competence

In interpersonal communication, communicative competence refers to the ability to communicate with others effectively and appropriately in one-on-one or small groups situations. Communication involves the use of both verbal and nonverbal communication skills to convey meaning and build relationships with others.

Some key components of communicative competence in interpersonal communication include:

Active listening: giving full attention to the speaker and demonstrating that you understand their perspective by reflecting back what they've said and asking clarifying questions

- **Nonverbal communication:** the use of body language, facial expressions, and tone of voice to convey meaning and build rapport with others
- **Empathy:** putting yourself in the other person's shoes and understanding their feelings and perspectives

- **Clarity and conciseness:** expressing ideas and feelings clearly and succinctly, avoiding ambiguity and confusion
- **Respect:** demonstrating appreciation for the other person's feelings, opinions, and perspectives, even if you disagree with them
- **Conflict resolution:** using communication skills to resolve conflicts and disagreements in a constructive and positive way

How Can You Improve Your Communicative Competence?

Developing communicative competence involves improving your ability to effectively and appropriately communicate with other people in different situations.

Active Listening

Improving your communicative competence involves learning to listen, which is surprisingly hard for some people. When another person is talking, many of us find ourselves in our own minds, either reviewing what we've just said or thinking about what we want to say next. In the process, we can totally blank out what the other person is saying. It's a total listening fail!

To become an active listener, you'll need to put your other thoughts out of your mind and focus all your attention upon what the speaker is saying as you try to understand their perspective. Avoid interrupting or jumping to conclusions, and ask clarifying questions if needed.

Becoming an active listener takes practice and effort, but you can employ several strategies to help improve your listening skills:

- **Pay attention:** Focus your attention on the speaker and eliminate distractions, such as your phone or other devices. Maintain eye contact with your roommate and give them your full attention.
- **Show interest:** Demonstrate interest in what your roommate is saying by nodding your head, asking questions, or providing feedback.
- **Paraphrase:** When a break occurs in their speaking and it's your turn, you can summarize or restate what your roommate has said in your own words to confirm your understanding.
- **Ask questions:** Ask open-ended questions to clarify information and show your roommate that you're interested in what they have to say.
- **Avoid interrupting:** Avoid interrupting your roommate and allow them to finish their thoughts before responding.
- **Provide feedback:** Provide feedback to your roommate, such as acknowledging their emotions or expressing empathy.
- **Practice mindfulness:** Focus on being present in the moment and listening without judgment.

Even though it's called "active listening," this activity involves more than just listening. It also involves providing nonverbal and sometimes verbal feedback along the way. Learn and practice responsiveness. Studies show that compassionate responsiveness ultimately enhances the quality of the relationship.

Verbal Communication Skills

To improve your verbal communication skills, develop your ability to express your thoughts and ideas clearly and effectively. Coupled with appropriate tone and body language, always try to approach a conversation with tact, diplomacy, and empathy.

If you're approaching a roommate with a concern, avoid confrontational language and avoid blaming. Put yourself in your roommate's shoes and be sensitive to their needs and feelings. When sharing your opinion, use "I" statements to avoid blaming or accusing the other person. For example, say "I feel" instead of "you did this." This helps to avoid placing blame, and instead it focuses on your personal feelings.

Tailor your language to the situation and the audience. Choose your words carefully, and choose your phrasing carefully, as well. Avoid any words that might be inflammatory or push your roommate's hot buttons, either hurting their feelings or making them angry. Problems remain unsolved when one party in the conversation feels hurt or angry, so your goal is to keep the conversation at an objective level—make it about the problem and not about the person. Try to solve the problem together, but don't ever make it your mission to "fix" the person, since that's not your role.

Learn and practice problem-solving skills, which can help you in many other settings in your life as well. Before you can solve a problem, you first need to define the problem together. Then, the two of you together can brainstorm solutions and consider all that come to mind. Next, evaluate the solutions based on their feasibility and potential effectiveness. Compare the pros and cons of each one to determine the best possible course of action. Finally, develop a plan for implementing that solution, determining the elements, responsibilities, and timeline you'll need.Top of Form

Nonverbal Communication Skills

The keys to enhancing your nonverbal communication skills include paying attention to your body language, gestures, eye contact, tone of voice, and facial expressions. Ensure that they're consistent with your verbal communication and convey your intended message. Nonverbal communication can complement, reinforce, or contradict the words we use in our verbal communication.

Below, some examples of nonverbal communication skills:

Facial expressions: The expressions on our faces can convey a wide range of emotions, such as happiness, sadness, anger, or surprise. Smiling, frowning, and making eye contact are all important aspects of facial expressions.

Research shows that some facial expressions are universal across cultures, while others may be culture-specific. Some examples include:

Universal facial expressions:

1. Happiness: A smile
2. Sadness: A frown

3. Anger: A scowl
4. Fear: A wide-eyed, open-mouthed expression
5. Disgust: A wrinkled nose and raised upper lip

Culture-specific facial expressions that vary across cultures:

1. Contempt (this expression involves a slight curl of the lip on one side of the mouth and is more commonly recognized in Western cultures)
2. Embarrassment
3. Shame
4. Surprise

It's important to be aware of both universal and culture-specific facial expressions when communicating with people from different backgrounds.

Body language: The way we hold ourselves and move our bodies can also communicate a lot about our thoughts and feelings. For example, crossing our arms can indicate defensiveness or discomfort, while standing up straight and making eye contact can convey confidence and engagement. Your body language isn't just how you're positioning your body; it also directs your energy toward a person or withholds your energy from the interaction. Be very aware of what your body is communicating during an interaction.

Also, be aware of touch behaviors. Some people are "huggers" and are very demonstrative with their hands and body, but it's always a good idea to obtain consent before touching another person, since touch is so loaded with conflicting meanings and can make many people extremely uncomfortable. Touch can, of course, convey sexual innuendos as well as friendly affection, but in a professional context, it can also be a form of harassment and an exercise of power. In today's sensitive environment, always ask first.

Gestures: Hand gestures, such as pointing or waving, can also convey important messages. The way we use our hands can emphasize certain points, demonstrate understanding, or convey enthusiasm. Be aware that symbolic hand gestures are culture-specific, and that certain gestures can have different meanings in different cultural contexts. In general, avoid pointing directly at people when you're talking to them, which can be seen as an aggressive act, and always be aware of what your hands may be "saying."

Tone of voice: The way we speak, including the tone, volume, and pace of our voice, can also convey important nonverbal messages. For example, a calm and soothing voice can indicate reassurance, while a raised voice can indicate anger or frustration. When you feel attacked or irritated after a conversation but can't understand why, examine the tone of voice the person used. Personally, a snarky, sarcastic, frustrated, or condescending tone of voice can make me feel very upset and put me on the defensive, even if the words a person uses aren't problematic.

Eye contact: This is an important aspect of nonverbal communication in our culture. In mainstream American society, it can indicate engagement, interest, and confidence. In the business world, the ideal (based on a particular model of an extraverted personality type) is someone who confidently makes and holds eye contact.

However, in many cultures around the world, including subcultures within the United States, making intense eye contact is perceived as being aggressive, exercising dominance, and disrespectful to other people. These include some African American, Asian, Latino, and Native American cultures.

Consider the animal world, in which holding eye contact demonstrates strength among many creatures, such as dogs, cats, bears, wolves, and primates. As such, it's a threat or challenge from a dominant member of the pack or group. Breaking eye contact, on the other hand, is a signal of submission.

Be aware that norms of eye contact vary enormously from culture to culture. In the dominant U.S. culture, avoiding eye contact may convey discomfort, disinterest, or dishonesty. However, many Americans find eye contact disconcerting. Introverts are much more likely to avoid eye contact than extraverts are, and people on the autism spectrum or who have social anxiety disorders usually find eye contact uncomfortable or stressful.

So if you're dealing with a roommate who avoids eye contact, try to understand the reason before making assumptions or judgments.

Cultural Sensitivity

Being culturally sensitive comes down to developing an understanding of different cultures and communication styles. Be sure that you're respectful of differences in communication patterns, including nonverbal cues, language use, and levels of formality.

Differences in cultures don't need to be marked by nationality. Of course, we assume that people from different nations have different cultural norms and traditions, but most multicultural countries contain many regional or ethnic cultures as well, including the United States.

If you have a roommate from a different region of the country, they can bring an unfamiliar culture into your household as well. They may also bring distinct cultural habits and traditions based upon their race, ethnicity, religion, or social class experience. You'll find differences between people raised in urban areas from those who grew up in small towns or rural areas, or from those growing up in the suburbs. We all have distinctly different lifestyles depending upon the cultures our parents brought into their marriages to form our family, as well as the cultural environments in which we grew up.

You'll no doubt experience cultural differences with each roommate you encounter, so being prepared to avoid ethnocentrism is essential. Ethnocentrism is the belief that your own ways of living and acting are the norm and are superior to the "odd" or "weird" ways that other people do things.

The most productive way to approach living with cultural differences in your roommate household is with an attitude of fascination and gratitude that you have the opportunity to learn about (and perhaps even experiment with) other cultural traditions. The most delicious of these involves eating the cuisine of another culture as you're exposed to new foods and flavors!

Emotional Intelligence

Build your ability to recognize and manage your own emotions in order to understand the emotions of others. This can help you communicate more effectively in emotionally charged situations and build stronger relationships. Show empathy by putting yourself in your roommate's shoes and trying to see things from their perspective. Acknowledge their feelings and validate their experiences, even if you don't agree with them. Be flexible by willing to compromise and make adjustments to your behavior and living arrangements to accommodate your roommate's needs. Remain open to feedback and willing to make changes to improve your relationship.

Conflict Resolution

Develop your ability to manage conflicts constructively by listening to others' perspectives, remaining calm, and finding mutually beneficial solutions. If conflicts arise, use problem-solving skills to find an end goal that suits everyone. Avoid blaming or attacking your roommate, and focus on finding a resolution that works for both of you.

When Things Go Poorly

Let's look at some examples of poor communication competence in a shared housing situation that can create tension, lead to conflict, and prompt a miserable living situation.

Avoiding Communication: Passive-Aggressive Behavior

Ignoring problems or refusing to communicate can create tension and misunderstandings. Try not to hide from your roommate to avoid having to confront them (or being confronted) when tension arises. Even though you may have a personality type that avoids conflict, failing to tackle a problem in a diplomatic way when it's small can result in a festering problem that becomes more and more toxic and unhealthy.

Being unresponsive or refusing to engage with the other person is another poor communication choice. Part of the implicit agreement when you take on the role of roommate (and hopefully made clear in the Roommate Agreement) is your responsibility to be willing and ready to communicate with your roommate.

If your roommate is aggressively demanding a response from you in the heat of the moment, you may need to take the lead and set up a time and place to have a house meeting so that the two of you can talk in a calmer and more defused setting. If necessary, ask a third person to act as a mediator if you believe your conversation with your roommate alone will break down.

Another culprit when it comes to evasion is relying on indirect communication, such as texting or leaving notes instead of having a face-to-face conversation, to do your emotional work. These are surefire ways to escalate the problem rather than solving it. Not only can terse texts or Post-it notes become easily misunderstood, but they can also cause confusion and resentment.

Passive-aggressive behavior is a form of indirect expression of hostility, negative attitudes, and resentment. It involves avoiding direct confrontation or communication while still expressing negative emotions toward a person or situation. These can erupt as emotional outbursts or pent-up verbal aggressions that are inappropriate and out of order in a roommate situation.

Be mindful of your own emotions and how they affect your behavior toward your roommate. Try to manage your emotions in a constructive way so that you can avoid negative emotional outbursts or passive-aggressive behavior.

Unclear Expectations

Vague or ambiguous communication, such as not clearly stating expectations or responsibilities, can lead to misunderstandings and conflicts. Long-term expectations should be part of your Roommate Agreement. Short-term expectations (let's say your roommate's sister is coming to visit from another state for a week and staying in your home) should be the subject of a dedicated conversation between yourself and your roommate about what each of you expects during that time and who will take responsibility for what.

Failure to Actively Listen—and Interrupting, Too

Constantly interrupting others is usually perceived as rude and can prevent effective communication. Even if you're eager to add something to what the other person is saying, be patient and let them finish saying what they need to.

Not actively listening to others and not responding to their concerns can lead to frustration and a breakdown in communication. Review the section on Active Listening in the previous section of this chapter.

Making assumptions about others' thoughts or feelings without verifying them can also lead to conflicts and misunderstandings. If you think you know what your roommate wants, how they feel about something, or whether they'll agree or disagree with a decision, ask them! Don't assume or second-guess. If you do, you may well be totally off-base.

Being Disrespectful of a Person or Their Boundaries

Being disrespectful or dismissive of others can cause hurt feelings and lead to a breakdown in communication. Violating someone's privacy or personal space and ignoring their boundaries is an all-too-frequent problem with roommates or housemates. I'm not necessarily talking about going through their drawers or reading their journals (although that happens, too—and shouldn't!). Honoring your roommate's right to privacy and alone time is one of the top considerations when you're sharing housing with someone.

If you're an extravert and your roommate is an introvert, they'll likely desire much more time alone than you will. If you expect your roommate or housemate to fulfill your social needs for constant companionship, you're in the wrong. You need to find other outlets to satisfy those needs. If you feel your introvert roommate resisting social invitations or pulling away from you to spend time alone in their own space, realize that those are their personal needs and not a rejection of you as a person. "I need my space" is a daily refrain for most introverts.

Being overly critical of or questioning a housemate's habits, behavior, or lifestyle—or making offensive comments—can be disrespectful and hurtful (see the Cultural Sensitivity section of this chapter above). Whether their habits are individual choices or cultural traditions they've embraced, it's not your place to question them unless you feel they're harmful to you.

If you do feel fearful of these habits or that they're disagreeable with you, first learn the facts, then calmly ask for a house meeting to discuss it. This might include issues about smoking, drugs, chemical usage, firearms, racist or homophobic comments, or bringing dangerous people into the house.

Disregarding shared responsibilities is also a form of disrespectful behavior. Not taking responsibility for shared tasks such as cleaning, paying bills, or maintaining the living space can build up and create resentment.

Being Manipulative

Manipulation is a form of behavior that a person uses to control or influence others in a way that benefits themselves and their own needs. Manipulators often use guilt as a tool to get others to do what they want. They may use excessive flattery or compliments to win over others. They might twist or distort the truth, play the victim to gain sympathy, or change their behavior or promises depending on the situation or person involved.

A manipulative housemate may try to make you doubt your own thoughts, feelings, or perceptions to gain control over you. They generally use intimidation and try to control what you do, who you see, or what you say. Manipulative people may also be unable to empathize with others or show concern for their feelings or needs.

If you suspect that a roommate is being manipulative, it's important to set boundaries and protect yourself from their behavior.

If you have a roommate who's only mildly manipulative, they may have modeled their behavior on a parent or family member and be unaware that their behavior is unacceptable and toxic. If you have a housemate who is a master manipulator with years of practice perfecting their act, then you may not be able to continue living with them if the discomfort level rises too high.

Some behaviors within the manipulative behavior range are narcissism, which, at an extreme, is a personality disorder (though people can have narcissistic qualities without being mentally ill), and gaslighting, a type of psychological manipulation in which one person tries to make the other feel self-doubt and confusion about what is really happening in a situation. Those who gaslight often try to gain and exercise power and control over another person by distorting their reality, causing them to question their own intuition and judgment.

You're now armed with the essential tools of the communicative trade—when it comes to coexisting harmoniously in a roommate housing situation, but also in the world in general. Go forth and communicate soundly, succinctly, and sublimely! When you keep in mind that most, if not all, of society's issues stem from lack of communication, you'll be better prepared and willing to communicate more effectively with others, including your roomies.

Faith Fuson

How To Address Tensions and Resolve Conflicts

NOW THAT YOU know everything about roommates, their personality types, and how to communicate effectively with them, this final chapter is about problem-solving. How do you deal with a roommate or housemate that you find unpredictable, challenging, or difficult? What if you like the person but find some of their habits mystifying or really hard to adjust to? You may have trouble living with another person because of personality differences, because of mental health issues on one or both of your parts or because of conflicting values and lifestyle choices.

Be aware that, although some people are by their very nature difficult, most interpersonal conflicts arise because the dynamics between two people (you and your roommate) create an uncomfortable situation. Once each of you is feeling the discomfort, how you respond to it (and therefore how you interact with the other person) can either work positively to proactively resolve the conflict or cause the discomfort to multiply and spiral downward until one or both of you become miserable.

Obviously, I want to help you gain some essential skills to put you in the first category. However, if you find yourself on that slippery downward spiral, if you both commit to trying some conflict resolution techniques, the relationship can likely be saved. However, if you believe the relationship is past the point of no return, then it's time to disengage from the negative emotional maelstrom and agree to part company as efficiently as possible, trying to keep things mature and professional as you take steps to go your separate ways.

Let's start with some ways you can contribute to trying to make your roommate relationship less uncomfortable. You may feel that the problem is entirely the other person's (that's the way that most of us tend to frame relationships that aren't ideal). But even if your roommate has habits that really annoy you or that you find to be difficult to live with, you can't expect them to read your mind and self-adjust their behavior to be the perfect roommate you've always dreamed of. In most cases, becoming a good partner in any situation requires a learning curve and adaptation by both parties to the needs and styles of the other.

If you find your roommate hard to get along with, the chapters in this book on personality types can be very helpful in understanding if your differences are based in having opposite personality traits. If you know your MBTI type and that of your roommate, you'll be able to see which of the four scales you may have in common, as well as which ones you diverge on. Those areas of divergence are usually the source of most roommate conflicts. Extraverts living with introverts, judgers living with perceivers, feelers living with thinkers—all these pairings can create very different ways of approaching the world, approaching problems, and interacting with others. Unless you become aware of this and realize, "Aha! Him seeming withdrawn is because he's an introvert, not because he's trying to avoid me," you'll probably build up resentment and even hostility after a while. This gradual accrual of negativity is what contributes to the downward spiral.

Mental Health Issues and Learning Disabilities

Occasionally, you may end up with a roommate whose personality issues may go beyond merely the personality types and preferences described them in this book. Statistically, as a young adult, you actually have a strong chance of finding a roommate who has mental health issues or learning disabilities.

According to, statistics from the U.S. National Institute of Mental Health an estimated 57.8 million adults aged 18 or older in the United States in 2021 had a mental health issue (which comprises any mental illness). This number represented 22.8% of all U.S. adults, but 33.7% of young adults aged 18-25. Serious mental illnesses affected 5.5% of all U.S. adults, but 11.4% of those were between the ages of 18 and 25. A serious mental illness (SMI) is defined as "a mental, behavioral, or emotional disorder resulting in serious functional impairment, which substantially interferes with or limits one or more major life activities."

The National Center for Health Statistics' National Health Interview Survey in 2020 found that 20.3% of adults had received mental health treatment in the previous year, including 16.5% who had taken prescription medication for their mental health, and 10.1% who received counseling or therapy from a mental health professional. The rates of taking ADHD, antidepressant, and psychotropic medication have steadily increased among adolescents and young adults during the past few decades.

Anxiety and depression are also two mental health conditions that can present with a range of symptoms. Below, some common characteristics of each:

Anxiety:

- Excessive worry or fear about everyday situations or events
- Difficulty controlling or stopping the worry
- Physical symptoms such as sweating, trembling, and racing heart
- Feeling on edge or irritable
- Avoiding situations or activities due to fear
- Panic attacks (sudden and intense episodes of fear or anxiety)

Depression:

- Persistent feeling of sadness or emptiness

- Loss of interest or pleasure in activities that were once enjoyed
- Changes in appetite and sleep patterns
- Difficulty concentrating or making decisions
- Fatigue and lack of energy
- Feelings of worthlessness or guilt
- Thoughts of death or suicide

It's important to note that not everyone experiences anxiety or depression in the same way, and that a person may display other symptoms or characteristics not listed here. If you or someone you know is experiencing symptoms of anxiety or depression, it's crucial to seek help from a mental health professional.

As a roommate or friend, you can play an important role in supporting someone who's dealing with anxiety or depression. The following are some ways you can provide support:

- **Listen actively:** One of the most important things you can do is to simply listen to your roommate without judgment or interruption. Give them your full attention and let them express themselves without feeling rushed or dismissed.
- **Be empathetic:** Let them know that you understand that they're going through a difficult time and that you're there to support them. Try to see things from their perspective, and acknowledge their feelings and experiences.
- **Offer practical help:** If they're struggling with everyday tasks or responsibilities, offer assistance in practical ways. This could mean running errands or cooking a meal.

- **Encourage self-care:** Motivate them to prioritize looking after themselves, in ways like getting enough sleep, eating healthy, and engaging in physical activity. Offer to join them for a walk or exercise class or share healthy meal ideas.
- **Avoid judgment or criticism:** Avoid making assumptions or judgments about their behavior or feelings. Remember that anxiety and depression are medical conditions, and that their experiences are valid and real.
- **Provide resources:** Offer information on mental health resources, such as therapy, support groups, or hotlines. Help them connect with resources in your community or online.
- **Check in regularly:** Keep in touch with your roommate and check in on them often. Let them know that you're there to support them, and that they can reach out to you whenever they need to.

Remember that providing support for someone with anxiety or depression can be challenging, and that it's important to take care of yourself as well. Make sure you're getting enough rest, exercise, and social support, and seek help if you need it.

One particular group of disorders that you may encounter involves people with autism spectrum disorders (ASD), which affect 1 to 2% of the population. As roommates, they may exhibit social impairments, communication difficulties, and repetitive behaviors, as well as anxiety and depression. These individuals, if properly diagnosed, should be receiving supportive services from family members, academic coaching and support services (if in college), or other agencies.

If you live with a roommate who has ASD, you can develop a positive living arrangement if you communicate openly and respectfully with them about how it impacts their daily life and how you can provide support. Learn as much as you can about autism spectrum disorder so that you'll understand how it can impact your roommate's behavior, communication, and social interactions. Also, it's important to avoid making assumptions or judgments about their behavior or abilities.

Discuss expectations for household chores, quiet hours, and other living arrangements. Establish clear boundaries and communicate them clearly to avoid misunderstandings or conflicts. Many people on the autism spectrum benefit from routine and structure. Respect your roommate's need for consistency and predictability in their daily life, and avoid sudden changes or surprises. Also, many people with ASD are sensitive to certain sounds, smells, or textures. Respect your roommate's sensory needs and avoid sensory stimuli that may be overwhelming or uncomfortable for them.

In addition to mental illnesses, another category of mental health includes learning disabilities. These refer to a group of disorders that impact a person's ability to acquire, process, and communicate information effectively. Although you're not necessarily directly involved in a classroom setting with your roommate, learning disabilities can have a significant impact on how individuals lead their daily lives.

Below are some of the most common learning disabilities and how they can affect a young adult's daily life:

Dyslexia: This condition affects a person's ability to read, write, and spell. It can make it challenging for young adults to comprehend written information, follow instructions, and communicate effectively. This can impact their academic performance, as well as their ability to participate in social activities that involve reading and writing.

Attention Deficit Hyperactivity Disorder (ADHD): This is a neurodevelopmental disorder that impacts a person's ability to focus, pay attention, and control their impulses. Young adults with ADHD may struggle to stay organized, manage their time effectively, and complete tasks. They may also have difficulty socializing, making friends, and maintaining relationships due to their impulsive behavior and lack of focus.

Dyscalculia: This is a learning disability that affects a person's ability to understand and work with numbers. The condition can make it challenging for young adults to perform basic arithmetic, understand mathematical concepts, and use money effectively. It can also impact their ability to navigate the world around them, such as understanding directions, telling time, and using a calendar.

Dysgraphia: This is another learning disability that affects a person's ability to write. Young adults with dysgraphia may struggle with handwriting, spelling, and grammar, which can make it challenging to communicate effectively in written form. This can impact their academic performance, as well as their ability to participate in social activities that involve writing.

Nonverbal Learning Disorder (NLD): This is a neurological disorder that impacts a person's ability to understand nonverbal cues, such as body language and facial expressions. It can make it challenging for young adults to interpret social situations, understand social norms, and make friends. NLD can also impact their ability to navigate the workplace and engage in professional relationships.

Living with a roommate who has learning disabilities can present unique challenges, but it's possible to develop a positive and supportive living arrangement. The following are six tips to help you live with a roommate who has learning disabilities:

1. **Communicate openly and respectfully:** Talk to your roommate about their learning disabilities and how they impact their daily life. Ask them what support or accommodations they need and how you can help. Listen to their needs and concerns with an open mind and a non-judgmental attitude.
2. **Be patient and understanding:** Living with a learning disability can be frustrating and challenging. Be patient and understanding when your roommate struggles with certain tasks or activities. Avoid making assumptions or judgments about their abilities based on their disability.
3. **Establish clear boundaries and expectations:** Discuss expectations for living arrangements such as shared cooking, finances, and household chores. Establish clear boundaries and communi-

cate them clearly to avoid misunderstandings or conflicts.
4. **Offer support and assistance:** Offer to help your roommate with tasks or activities they may find challenging due to their learning disability. For example, you could offer to proofread their written work or help them stay organized. Make sure you're respecting their independence and autonomy while providing support.
5. **Respect their privacy and personal space:** Everyone needs their personal space and privacy, and this is especially true for someone living with a learning disability. Respect your roommate's privacy and boundaries, and avoid sharing personal information about them with others without their permission.
6. **Celebrate their strengths and accomplishments:** If your roommate has a learning disability, it's vital to recognize and celebrate their strengths and accomplishments. Encourage them to pursue their interests and hobbies, and offer positive reinforcement when they achieve their goals.

Conflicting Lifestyle Choices

Beyond personality or medically diagnosable conditions, your disagreeable or annoying roommate situation may be due to their lifestyle choices that clash with yours or that contribute to behaviors on their part that you find unbearable.

These can include drug usage, whether legal or illegal, as well as excessive alcohol consumption. Frankly, these are issues that you and your potential roommate should address in your initial interview before ever agreeing to move in together, but we know that not everyone is willing to acknowledge their degree of dependency on these substances, nor the effects the substances have on their own behavior.

Living with a roommate who drinks heavily or uses drugs can be a difficult and stressful situation. Below, six tips to help you deal with this situation:

1. **Set clear boundaries:** Let your roommate know that you're uncomfortable with their behavior and that you have certain boundaries. For example, you can ask them not to use drugs or drink excessively in your shared living spaces or not to invite people over who engage in this behavior.
2. **Communicate openly and calmly:** When talking to your roommate, try to stay calm and non-judgmental. Avoid using accusatory language or blaming them for their behavior. Instead, express your concerns and ask for their input on how to address the situation.
3. **Avoid enabling their behavior:** If your roommate asks you to buy or supply drugs or alcohol for them, refuse to do so. This may not only be illegal but will also encourage their destructive and harmful habit.
4. **Seek support from others:** If you're struggling to cope with your roommate's behavior, seek support from friends, family members, or a mental health professional. They can provide you with guidance and support to help you manage your stress and anxiety.

5. **Know your options:** If your roommate's behavior is putting your safety or well-being at risk, you may need to consider finding a new living situation if things become unbearable.
6. **Take care of yourself:** Living with someone who drinks heavily or uses drugs can be emotionally taxing. Take care of yourself by eating well, getting enough sleep, and engaging in activities that bring you joy.

A similar situation that I've experienced is having a roommate or housemate who engages in frequent, *casual hook-up sexual behavior* with strangers. Again, it's not your responsibility to judge your roommate's morality or change what they get up to, but bringing strangers into your shared home for the purpose of sex is a dangerous proposition—not only for your roommate but also for you and anyone else living in the house.

Please understand that I'm not talking about having a roommate who is in a sexual relationship and brings home a significant other for a sleepover now and then. I'm talking about nearly anonymous sex-only hookups with people your roommate doesn't really know anything about. This is where your Roommate Agreement comes into play, and perhaps a house meeting needs to be held to clarify the ground rules for the sake of the physical and material safety of household members. Situations like this call for either "getting a room" or going to the other person's place to do the deed.

What To Do If You Just Don't Get Along

What I'll share with you here are the things you can do, on your end, to try to turn a shared housing situation that hasn't gotten off on the right foot into one that's at least bearable—and, hopefully, one that can grow and flourish with an infusion of improved communication.

So: you're not getting along with your roommate. First, let's try to determine why. What I'd like for you to do is to list the reasons you believe the two of you are having trouble living together.

Before you get too far, let me help you with the phrasing. We tend to start such lists with "She's..." or "He's...," as in "She's really opinionated and won't listen to me" or "He's very self-absorbed and seems oblivious to what's going on in our house." Before you add too many items like this to your list, I want you to turn around the phrasing to make them "I" statements instead. Focus on how your roommate's behaviors make you feel:

"I feel disrespected and ignored when she seems to not listen to me but instead insists upon doing things her own way."

"I feel that I end up taking responsibility for things because he's not stepping up to be an equal partner in our household."

This may seem hard at first, but learning to rephrase issues in terms of how they affect you rather than in words that blame or judge another person is an essential step toward improving communication in a relationship.

Communication is crucial, so the best way to proactively avoid that downward spiral that leads to the point of no return is to set up a time to talk as soon as you feel those first pangs of discomfort. Discomfort and disagreements are a natural part of any relationship, but how you handle them can make all the difference.

The following are seven tips for sitting down and talking through tension or a disagreement with someone:

1. **Stay calm:** It's important to remain levelheaded and avoid getting defensive or aggressive when discussing what's bothering you. Take a few deep breaths or a break if you need to before continuing the conversation.
2. **Listen actively:** Listen to the other person's point of view and try to understand where they're coming from. Repeat back what they're saying to show that you're listening and to make sure you understand their perspective.
3. **Express your feelings:** Use "I" statements to express how you're feeling about the situation. For example, say "I feel hurt when you..." instead of "You always make me feel...". This helps the other person understand how their actions are affecting you.
4. **Avoid blame and criticism:** Avoid blaming the other person or criticizing them for their behavior or actions. Instead, focus on the issue at hand and how you can work together to resolve it.
5. **Find common ground:** Look for areas of agreement or common ground to help move the con-

versation forward. This could be something as simple as both of you wanting the same outcome. Finding common ground is often the turning point that flips a downward-heading relationship upward again.
6. **Brainstorm solutions:** Work together to come up with potential solutions that work for both of you. Be open to compromise and try to find a solution that meets both of your needs.
7. **Follow up:** After you've had your conversation about the disagreement, revisit the issue with the other person to ensure that you're both on the same page. If necessary, make a plan to check in with each other again in the future to make sure that the issue is resolved.

Remember, disagreements are a natural part of any relationship, and it's important to work through them in a respectful and constructive way. By following the steps above, you can talk through a disagreement in a way that will potentially strengthen your relationship.

Conflict resolution can take place at many levels and in a huge range of situations. Often, minor interpersonal conflict can be handled using the methods outlined above.

If the conflict has lasted longer, festered, or become really toxic, you may need to decide if the relationship is salvageable or not. If you and your roommate both want to try to work out your differences, then using a conflict resolution process is your best bet for working through the problems yourselves. It'll take a dedicated effort from each of you, but you can definitely achieve a resolution if you want it and are willing to work collaboratively to make it happen.

The main principles of conflict resolution are:

1. **Respect:** This is key to conflict resolution. It's important to treat the other person with respect, even if you disagree with them.
2. **Empathy:** This is the ability to put yourself in someone else's shoes and understand how they're feeling. Empathy can help you to better understand the other person's perspective and find a solution that works for both parties.
3. **Understanding:** It's vital to try to understand the other person's point of view, even if it differs from yours. This can help you find common ground and work toward a solution.
4. **Communication:** Proper communication is essential for conflict resolution. It's necessary to express your thoughts and feelings clearly and to actively listen to the other person's perspective.
5. **Collaboration:** This principle involves working together to find a solution that meets the needs of both parties. It requires compromise and a willingness to find common ground.
6. **Creativity:** Sometimes, finding a solution to a conflict requires thinking outside the box and coming up with creative solutions.
7. **Persistence:** Conflict resolution can take time and effort, so it's important to be persistent and not give up, even if the process is challenging.

In some very difficult cases, you may need to find a third party to serve as a mediator or advisor to your conflict resolution process. If you're in college, a counselor on your campus will likely offer free counseling sessions as part of your student services. Finding someone to mediate a conflict resolution can depend on the situation and the parties involved. Below, some ways to find a mediator:

- Ask friends, family members, colleagues, or other trusted individuals if they know of any mediators who may be able to help. They may have worked with a mediator in the past or know someone who currently does.
- A quick online search can often provide a list of mediators in your area. Be sure to read reviews and do your research before selecting someone.
- Check with professional organizations, such as the American Bar Association or the Association for Conflict Resolution, which may have directories or resources for finding a mediator in your area.
- Many cities have community mediation centers that provide free or low-cost mediation services. Contacting them may be a good option, especially if cost is a concern.
- If the conflict involves legal issues, working with a lawyer may be necessary. They might be able to recommend a mediator or provide mediation services themselves.

When selecting a mediator, it's important to find someone neutral, unbiased, and experienced in conflict resolution. It's also essential to ensure that both parties are comfortable with the mediator and agree to work with them.

When It's Time to End the Relationship and Live Separately

While most bad roommate situations can generally be resolved through communication and conflict resolution skills, not every person involved is always willing to put in the effort. Also, some situations arise when living together becomes dangerous or traumatic and it's clearly time to separate yourself without question. In those cases, how do you end a shared housing situation?

Remember what's been mentioned numerous times throughout this book—a roommate relationship is a business relationship. Don't approach the separation as if you're breaking up a friendship or getting a divorce. You're ending a business partnership—so if you keep it businesslike, everything will go much more smoothly. You have no need to express anger or resentment or cast blame. All you need to say is, "This living situation isn't working out, so we need to end this shared housing arrangement."

- A lot will depend upon the legal status of how you came to be living together.
- If you're sharing a dormitory room on campus and you find yourselves unable to continue living together, you'll need to contact your university's residence or housing office to request being reassigned.
- If you're sharing a house or apartment and both of you have your names on the lease, you'll need to check the terms of the lease to find out if one of you is able to move out and sublet your space. If this is

permitted, you and your roommate will need to decide who will move out and how the remaining roommate will find a replacement. You'll both be responsible financially until all terms of the lease are legally transferred to the new person.
- If you're sharing a house or apartment in both your names ("jointly and severally liable") but the lease doesn't allow subletting, you'll need to talk with your landlord and may need to obtain legal advice about the tenant laws of your state.
- If the lease is in only one person's name, or if one roommate owns the home and the roommate who's leaving is renting from the other roommate, then make sure that all legal obligations are fulfilled and all debts are paid as per the terms in your rental agreement.

Whenever roommates separate or joint tenancy ends, it's essential that each person holds up their end of the financial agreement. Try to separate your emotions and bad feelings from the business end of the relationship. No matter how much you may dislike the other person, protect your own integrity and legal record by being accountable and responsible for all your debts. Unfortunately, when people leave on bad terms, they often try to shirk their responsibilities, sometimes in vengeance. They may leave their room or the house in disarray, for example, or they may leave without paying their share of the utility bill.

If you sustain a substantial loss from a vindictive roommate's walking out on responsibilities, you can take them to small claims court. Otherwise, you may need to accept that you might never recover the funds.

Faith Fuson

Final Words

ULTIMATELY, LIVING WITH a roommate or housemate should be a rewarding and enriching experience that persuades you of the ultimate goodness of humans who can co-exist in harmony and who try to be their best selves around each other.

While you'll occasionally encounter a situation that's unsustainable, as discussed above, the majority of roommate relationships will thrive if you apply the guidance provided in this book and have a partner who's willing to put forth the effort to make things work.

As you develop and use your emotional intelligence, communicative competence, and knowledge of personality types, you can expect to see the quality of your roommate relationship blossom.

With the use of the Roommate Agreement, as well as setting aside regular times for house meetings, you and your housemate will learn to iron out any wrinkles before they become engrained creases in your relationship.

You'll also learn to adapt your expectations as you become more aware of your roommate's preferences, strengths, and weaknesses—and vice versa—making each of you a more tolerant and understanding member of the shared household and becoming more willing to occasionally pick up the slack for each other.

For most of us, enjoying the mutual support system of having a roommate—as well as its economic and security benefits—makes the process of learning to collaborate with another person worthwhile. If you approach the partnership with respect, maturity, and professionalism—including a willingness to collaborate and communicate with one another's best interests in mind—you'll form a harmonious living arrangement that serves the domestic desires of everyone under the same shared roof.

Refer to this book often, follow its guidelines, and enjoy all the peaks and valleys (but hopefully more peaks!) of a fruitful shared living arrangement.

Faith Fuson

Bonus Content

READY TO TAKE your roommating game to legendary status? Unlock the secrets of harmonious cohabitation with our Free Roommate Agreement! Scan this QR code! It's time to level up your roommating skills and make your living space the envy of all! Free Bonus Roommate Agreement

Tired of playing the never-ending game of "Whose turn is it to clean"? Let's end the cleaning chaos and embrace domestic harmony with our free and fully customizable Roommate Cleaning Checklist! Together, we can conquer the dust bunnies, defeat the dirty dishes, and create an Instagram-worthy living space. It's time to unleash your inner cleaning ninja and bring peace to your shared abode. Grab your free cleaning checklist now because a clean home is a happy home (and less mess means more time for Netflix marathons and dance parties)! Let's make cleaning fun again! Free Bonus Roommate Cleaning Checklist.

If this book has helped you navigate the treacherous seas of roommating and made your college experience a little less sucky, don't keep it to yourself! Share your newfound wisdom with the world by leaving a review that would make Shakespeare proud (or at least chuckle). Let's spread the roommate love and make sure no one else has to suffer through microwave mishaps and passive-aggressive sticky notes. Get those typing fingers ready and show some love for The College Roommate Essentials book, because together, we can conquer the realm of roommating!

Thank you - Faith Fuson

Faith Fuson

Made in the USA
Las Vegas, NV
15 December 2023